PRAYERS FOR USE AT THE ALTERNATIVE SERVICES

PRAYERS FOR USE AT THE ALTERNATIVE SERVICES

Compiled and adapted from
Ancient, Medieval and Modern Sources

by

DAVID SILK
Archdeacon of Leicester

Foreword by

Canon Frank Colquhoun

MOWBRAY
LONDON & OXFORD

ISBN 0 264 66483 3 (hardback)
ISBN 0 264 66711 5 (special binding)

First published in 1980 by A. R. Mowbray & Co Ltd
Saint Thomas House, Becket Street, Oxford, OX1 1SJ

Text set in 9/10 pt Linotron 202 Palatino, printed and bound in Great Britain at The Pitman Press, Bath

To TREVOR JALLAND
ARTHUR COURATIN
and COLIN BUCHANAN
this book is dedicated
with gratitude
and affection

CONTENTS

FOREWORD

The publication of *The Alternative Service Book 1980* is a major event in the life of the Church of England. It is the Church's first completely new prayer book since the Reformation, and the first to provide forms of worship in the language of the twentieth rather than the sixteenth century.

This a matter for which we must be duly thankful, for the language of worship is important. Two reasons among many may be mentioned. In the first place a fundamental principle is at stake. Scripture teaches us to love and worship God with all our mind as well as with all our heart; to pray and sing with the understanding as well as with the spirit. This requires that the language of our services should be intelligible and such as 'is most easy and plain for the understanding', as Cranmer put it.

Secondly, public prayer provides a pattern of prayer and has a teaching value. People's ideas about prayer in general are influenced by the sort of prayers they hear in church. If the language is archaic and obscure, prayer itself tends to be regarded as something antiquated, remote, unreal. On the other hand if the language is simple and natural, and closely related to the everyday world in which we live, people will get an impression of the reality and relevance of prayer as far as their own lives are concerned.

The present collection of prayers, designed to serve as a companion and supplement to the new service book, rightly adopts a contemporary idiom. It gains considerably by being arranged under the headings of the principal services and in relation to the Church's new calendar and lectionary. Another gain is that the prayers are drawn from a variety of sources and cover a wide field. And an excellent index is provided.

The result is a book which I feel sure will be of considerable assistance to clergy and others in their endeavours to order today's worship in accordance with today's needs.

Frank Colquhoun

INTRODUCTION

This collection of prayers is intended to serve as a companion volume to *The Alternative Service Book 1980*. That book provides for the Church of England a complete series of services for public worship alternative to those contained in the Book of Common Prayer (1662). As the first English Prayer Book of 1549 adopted the use of the 'vulgar tongue', that is the language currently in use in England in the sixteenth century, so the Alternative Service Book adopts language which reflects modern usage, particularly in the almost invariable use of the 'you' form of address to God. In that sense the Alternative Service Book may be regarded as an 'updated Book of Common Prayer', but in another respect it is a book quite different in ethos and character. Above all else it differs from the Book of Common Prayer in its provision of a broad scope for the discretion of the minister, both in the choice of alternatives and in the use of his own words. Thus, while its rubrics recognise and encourage the long-standing practice of using additional prayers after Morning and Evening Prayer, they also continue the more recent permission in the alternative services by providing in the Eucharist, as well as in the Marriage and Funeral services, the opportunity for the minister to use his own words. Indeed, in the Marriage service the couple may write or select prayers of their own. Furthermore, the provision of a 'Service without Communion' on the eucharistic model suggests a ground-plan for Family services and occasional acts of worship.

This comparatively recent departure from traditional Anglican practice, together with the wide use of variations in, or additions to, the statutory services according to season, seems to imply the need for a book of prayers to supplement the diet offered by the Alternative Service Book. In offering such a book I am only too conscious that others have contributed a vast amount of suitable material before me. I owe an enormous debt to Canon Frank Colquhoun, the compiler of *Parish Prayers* and *Contemporary Parish Prayers*, and acknowledge that the present volume has drawn on the latter considerably. I have also consulted and used prayers from many other sources, which are identified on pages 147–149.

In the provision of the Alternative Service Book the Liturgical Commission has adopted prayers from three distinct sources. First, it has looked at the originals in the ancient liturgies and translated or paraphrased them; secondly, it has used many of the well-known prayers from the Book of Common Prayer, or similar sources, and subjected them to modernisation by conservative revision, thus retaining many familiar phrases which have a slightly archaic ring; thirdly, it has prepared totally new material. The present volume has been compiled on the same principles.

Where prayers have been composed in Greek or Latin, I have generally gone back to the originals and attempted a new translation. At the outset this seemed likely to be a satisfactory approach, but it soon became clear that the imagery and thrust of many ancient prayers were not apt to the twentieth-century mind, and the translations began to be paraphrases. In some cases the prayers had to be abandoned. It was not just a matter of asking questions about the suitability of using the relative clauses characteristic of the Latin prayers, so resonantly translated by Cranmer, or even a problem of finding new ways to express eternal truths, but of asking whether or not the approach to God as a liege-lord, or the cruder assumptions about a personal devil, were likely to be of much use to the members of our congregations.

Where prayers have been adopted from earlier

English usage, either in familiar translations of older prayers, or from the work of English liturgiologists, I have altered as little as possible. As General Synod confined itself to conservative revision in such cases, so I have tended to retain archaisms where they were not unintelligible, or where they succinctly expressed an idea which a modern paraphrase would deprive of some meaning.

Where prayers have been adopted from modern English sources I have been content to make such changes as seemed necessary to remain congruous with Anglican doctrine, or to change the thrust of the prayer from, say, petition to intercession. All such changes are signified by an asterisk * against the name of the source, as are changes dictated by substituting 'you' for 'thou'. In particular it has not been easy to include some of the incomparable work of Eric Milner-White, although no collection of prayers would be complete without a contribution from him, especially at Passiontide. I have, however, used some of his prayers, but with as little adaptation as possible.

Some prayers have no ascription. They are drawn from my private collection, or from other published collections, and their authorship is unknown; if by their use I have infringed copyright, or failed to make acknowledgement, I apologise. Some prayers I have ventured to ascribe to myself; the ascription is only made where there is some claim to originality. However, I have been helped and nourished by so much material over the years that, even in this case, I suspect that there are echoes of the work of others.

The primary arrangement of the book is under the headings of the main services. Use of the indices will allow the ready transfer of much material from one service to another; for example, much of the provision for Morning and Evening Prayer will be useful at the eucharistic intercession for those who wish to avail themselves of the option of free prayer at that point. Traditional commemorations of the hours and seasons are offered for Morning and Evening Prayer, and these include responses, since the clergy may well wish to use them when they say the office together. After the main services there is a group of other prayers which experience suggests might be helpful, but which do not conveniently fall into the main categories. These prayers can be adapted for use at the statutory services, but, in the arrangement of this book, require a disproportionate space in the main sections.

The secondary arrangement of the book places the bulk of the material in relation to the Sundays and major Holy days. This method has been chosen to allow the clergy and readers the use of a wide variety of prayers in the course of the year, and to help those who are called upon without much notice to offer prayer to find material which is related to the themes of the year. Each package of prayers derives its thrust from the readings of the day, and thus secures the balance of subject matter achieved by the Alternative Calendar and Lectionary. It may appear that this arrangement is unduly restrictive, but recourse to the indices, and a careful wording of prefatory biddings, will relieve such restriction.

To offer help to all the churches in our parishes it has been necessary to include material representative of the entire spectrum of Anglican churchmanship. Among the sources are John Calvin and the Roman Missal, which, of course, contains a vast amount of material in modern English. However, churches which do not pray for the departed, or use Ashes on the first day of Lent, will often find it easy to adapt the prayers to their own liturgical tradition.

In provision for the Saints' Days I have made no attempt to offer a prayer for each festival and commemoration. One or two festivals of the Prayer Book

Calendar are supplied with prayers which, I hope, are suitable and helpful, and one or two typical saints have been selected. For example, the prayer for Thomas More's day, written around words which are well-known, may well speak for us on the festivals of Christians on both sides in the Reformation controversies, and, indeed, in more than one contemporary commemoration. The patron saints of the British Isles have been provided for, and the matter left there, since many prayers from the body of the book will be suitable.

The task of gathering and editing the material has consumed more time than I at first imagined, and my thanks are due to my wife, who has been tolerant of inroads into the sacred day off, and who has undertaken the considerable work of typing the manuscript. Moreover, I owe a considerable debt to my assistant at St George's, Beckenham, the Reverend J. R. Bartlett, who has both relieved me of some of my share of the parish work over the past months, and offered many helpful suggestions.

Here then is a further offering to those who wish to use the Alternative Service Book while being reluctant to abandon the rich resources of the past; it does not pretend to be comprehensive, but, used in conjunction with what is already available in the Alternative Service Book, and in the many books of supplementary prayers which are widely available, it may prove a helpful addition to the little libraries which we clergy accumulate in our stalls in church. That, at any rate, is my hope and prayer.

David Silk
The Feast of Saints Peter and Paul 1979

MORNING AND EVENING PRAYER

MORNING AND EVENING PRAYER

The Hours of the Day

EARLY MORNING

1 Eternal Jesus, in the early morning you offered yourself to the scorn and insults of your enemies; at this same hour give us, we pray, your grace and your mercy, that throughout this day we may find joy and peace in all that serves your praise and glory, for you are now alive, and reign with the Father and the Holy Spirit, God for ever and ever.

Prime

2 We give you heartfelt thanks, heavenly Father, for the rest of the past night, and for the gift of a new day with its opportunities of living to your glory. May we so pass its hours in the perfect freedom of your service that, when evening comes, we may again give you thanks; through Jesus Christ our Lord. *Daybreak Office of the Orthodox Church*

3 Into your hands, merciful Lord, we commend ourselves for this day; may we be aware of your presence until its end; remind us that in whatever good we do we are serving you; make us careful and watchful, so that in everything we may discern your will, and, knowing it, may gladly obey, to the honour and glory of your name; through Jesus Christ our Lord. *Gelasian Sacramentary*

4 God of love, the true sun of the world, eternally risen and never going down; in your mercy shine into our hearts, that the night of sin and the mists of error being banished, we may, this day and all our life, walk without stumbling along the way which you have set before us; through your Son Jesus Christ our Lord. *Erasmus*

MORNING

5 *I will pour out my Spirit on all mankind.*
The love of God has been poured into our hearts;
By the Holy Spirit which has been given to us.
God, our almighty Father, renew our hearts and minds by the power of the Holy Spirit, who strengthened your apostles at the third hour; through Christ our Lord. *Terce*

6 *Like a lamb that is led to the slaughter, and like a sheep that before its shearers is dumb, so he opened not his mouth.*
It was the third hour;
And they crucified him.
Lord Jesus Christ, Son of the living God, at the third hour you were led out to the pain of the cross for the salvation of the world; by the virtue of your saving passion blot out our sins and bring us to the glory of your eternal joy, for you are alive and reign, God, now and for ever. *Terce*

MID-DAY

7 *When I am lifted up from the earth, I will draw all men to myself.*
Jesus, remember me;
When you come in your kingly power.

Most gracious Jesus, our Lord and our God, who at this hour bore our sins in your body on the tree that we might die to sin and live to righteousness; have mercy on us, now and at the hour of death, and grant us, with all your people who now recall your saving passion, a holy and peaceful life in this world, and, through your grace, eternal glory in the life to come, where, with the Father and the Holy Spirit, you are alive and reign, one God, now and for ever. *Sext*

AFTERNOON

8 *When he suffered, he did not threaten; but he trusted to him who judges justly.*

Even here your hand shall lead me;
And your right hand shall hold me.

Hear us, merciful Jesus, and remember the hour in which you commended your spirit into the hands of your heavenly Father; by this your most precious death help us, that, being dead to the world, we may live to you alone; and that, at the hour of leaving this mortal life, we may be received into your eternal kingdom, there to reign with you, for ever and ever. *None*

9 Lord Jesus Christ, Son of the living God, set your passion, cross and death between your judgement and us, now and at the hour of our death. Give mercy and grace to the living, rest to the dead, to your holy Church peace and concord, and to us sinners eternal life and glory, for you are alive and reign with the Father and the Holy Spirit, one God, now and for ever. *None*

10 Gracious Lord Jesus, who died on the cross for us;

remember all who are sick and dying. May they neglect nothing which is necessary to making their peace with you before they die; save them from the snares of sin and evil; and bring them to a happy end; for the sake of your loving mercy. *None*

EVENING

11 Lord Jesus Christ, Son of the living God, at this evening hour you lay in the tomb and so hallowed the grave to be a bed of hope for all who trust you; give us sorrow for our sins which were the cause of your passion, that, when our bodies lie in the dust, our souls may live with you, for you are now alive, and reign with the Father and the Holy Spirit, one God, now and for ever. *Compline*

12 Be with us, merciful God, and protect us through the silent hours of this night, that we who are wearied by the changes and chances of this fleeting world, may rest upon your eternal changelessness; through Jesus Christ our Lord. *Leonine Sacramentary*

13 Look down, Lord, from your throne in heaven; let the light of your presence dispel the shadows of the night, and from the children of light banish the deeds of darkness; through Jesus Christ our Lord. *Compline*

14 Watch, dear Lord, with those who wake, or watch, or weep tonight, and let your angels protect those who sleep. Tend the sick. Refresh the weary. Sustain the dying. Calm the suffering. Pity the distressed. We ask this for the sake of your love. *Saint Augustine*

The Days of the Week

MONDAY

15 The Trinity

Holy, holy, holy, is the Lord God Almighty, who was and is and is to come.

Let us bless the Father, the Son, and the Holy Spirit;

Let us praise him and exalt him for ever.

Almighty and eternal God, strengthen our faith that we may firmly believe and truthfully proclaim the Trinity in this world, and, in the world to come, may perfectly know and joyfully behold you, face to face; for you live and reign, one God, now and for ever.

The Priest's Book of Private Devotion

16 The Faithful Departed

I heard a voice from heaven saying, write this; blessed are the dead who die in the Lord henceforth. Blessed indeed, says the Spirit, that they may rest from their labours.

I believe that I shall surely see the goodness of the Lord;

In the land of the living.

Almighty God, to whom all live; we remember all who have left this life in the hope of the resurrection, especially our families and friends, and those who have done us good: according to your promises, grant them refreshment, light and peace where there shall be no more mourning nor crying nor pain, and you will be our light for ever and ever.

The Priest's Book of Private Devotion

TUESDAY

17 The Holy Spirit

Come, Holy Spirit, fill the hearts of your faithful people, and kindle in them the fire of your love.

You send forth your Spirit and they are created;
And you renew the face of the earth.

Lord God, heavenly Father, may the Comforter who proceeds from you enlighten our minds, lead us into all truth, and make us active in your service; through Christ our Lord. *Gelasian Sacramentary*

18 The Name of Jesus

At the name of Jesus every knee shall bow, in heaven and on earth and under the earth.

There is no other name under heaven given among men;
By which we must be saved.

Heavenly Father, who in the naming of your incarnate Son Jesus declared the purpose of salvation to the whole world; grant that every tongue may confess that Jesus Christ is Lord, to your eternal glory; through the same Jesus Christ our Lord.

K. T. Street

WEDNESDAY

19 The Saints

How glorious is the kingdom, where all the saints rejoice with Christ; they are clothed in white robes and follow the Lamb wherever he goes.

The sounds of joy and deliverance;
Are in the tents of the righteous.

Almighty and everlasting God, you have kindled the flame of love in the hearts of the saints; grant to us the same faith and power of love, that, as we rejoice in their triumphs, we may be sustained by their example and fellowship; through Christ our Lord. *Gothic Missal*

20 The Angels

The angel of the Lord encamps around those who fear him, and delivers them in their need.

Praise the Lord, all you his hosts;
His servants who do his will.

Father in heaven, in all times of our testing and trial send your angels to strengthen and support us, that the prince of darkness may have no power over us; through Christ our Lord. *David Silk*

THURSDAY

21 The Eucharist

O sacred feast in which we partake of Christ, his sufferings are remembered, our minds are filled with his grace and we receive a pledge of the glory that is to be ours.

The Lord gave them the grain of heaven;
So men ate the bread of angels.

God our Father, whose Son at table offered himself as the innocent Lamb, and gave us this memorial of his passion until the end of time; feed your people and strengthen them in holiness, that the family of mankind may live in the light of one faith in one communion of love; through the same Christ our Lord.

22 Christ the High Priest

Since we have a great high priest who has passed through the heavens, Jesus the Son of God, let us hold fast our confession.

By a single offering;
He has perfected for all time those who are sanctified.

Lord God, who for your glory and our salvation made your Son to be a high priest for ever; grant that we who are freed from our sins by his blood may serve you acceptably as kings and priests in your new temple; through the same Christ our Lord. *David Silk*

FRIDAY

23 The Passion of Christ

Hail, our king, you alone have pity on our sinfulness.

Obedient to the Father you were led to be crucified;

As a meek lamb to the slaughter.

Lord Jesus Christ, who from the glorious presence of the Father came to earth, and shed your precious blood for the forgiveness of our sins; we pray that in the day of judgement we may hear you say, Come, blessed of my Father; and be worthy to stand at your right hand, for you are now alive and reigning with the same Father and the Holy Spirit, God now and for ever.

24 The Cross

The only thing about which I can boast is the cross of our Lord Jesus Christ, through whom the world is crucified to me, and I to the world.

For us Christ emptied himself and accepted death;

Even death on a cross.

Lord Jesus Christ, for the salvation of mankind you went up to the cross to give light to the world which was in darkness; shed that light on us, we pray, that we may come to eternal light, and, through the merits of your passion, enjoy life with you in heaven, for you are alive and reigning now and for ever.

SATURDAY

25 The Incarnation

A hallowed day has dawned upon us. Come and worship the Lord, for a great light has shone on the earth.

Blessed are you, Virgin Mary;

For you gave birth to the creator of all things.

Almighty and everlasting God, you have stooped to raise fallen humanity by the child-bearing of blessed Mary; grant that we who have seen your glory revealed in our human nature, and your love made perfect in our weakness, may daily be renewed in your image, and conformed to the pattern of your Son, Jesus Christ our Lord. *David Silk*

26 Baptism

Put on the new man, created in the image of God, in justice and in the holiness of truth.

Once you were darkness;

Now you are light in the Lord.

Lord God, by our baptism into the death and resurrection of your Son Jesus Christ we have been born again to be your children and heirs of eternal life; strengthen us by your Spirit to live in newness of life all our days; through the same Christ our Lord. *David Silk*

The Seasons of the Year

ADVENT

27 *The night is far gone, the day is at hand: let us then cast off the works of darkness, and put on the armour of light.*

Restore us again, O Lord of hosts;
Show us the light of your countenance and we shall be saved.

Almighty God, you sent your Son to redeem mankind, and will send him again to be our judge; may we so imitate him in the humility and purity of his first coming, that, when he comes again, we may be ready to greet him with joyful love and firm faith; through the same Christ our Lord.

28 Stir up your power, Lord, and with great might come among us; and, because we are sorely hindered by our sins, let your bountiful grace and mercy speedily help and deliver us; through Jesus Christ our Lord. *Gelasian Sacramentary*

CHRISTMAS

29 *Glory to God in the highest, and on earth peace among men with whom he is well pleased.*

Mercy and truth are met together;
Righteousness and peace have kissed each other.

Almighty God, you have shed upon us the new light of your incarnate Word, giving us gladness in our sorrow and a presence in our isolation; fill our lives with your light until they overflow with gladness and praise; through Christ our Lord.

30 Father eternal, cleanse and renew us each day by

the power of your Spirit, that the goodness of the incarnate Lord may be seen in our lives; fill the Church, and the whole world, with the light, joy, and peace of his birth, that his second coming in glory may be hastened, and all creation perfected in his eternal kingdom; through the same Jesus Christ our Saviour.

EPIPHANY

31 *Arise, shine, for your light has come, and the glory of the Lord has risen upon you.*

All kings shall fall down before him;
All nations shall do him service.

Almighty and everlasting God, you have revealed the incarnation of your Son by the bright shining of a star, which the wise men saw, and offered costly gifts in adoration; let the star of your justice always shine in our hearts, that we may give as our treasure all that we are and all that we possess, to your service; through Jesus Christ our Lord.

Gelasian Sacramentary

32 God, through your only Son you have hallowed the water of baptism to bring us to a new birth, and anointed him with your Spirit in the descent of the dove; keep your Church always safe from evil, direct our lives, and open the door of your kingdom to all who are waiting to enter; through Jesus our Messiah and Lord.

LENT

33 *Now is the acceptable time; now is the day of salvation; let us commend ourselves as servants of God through great* *endurance, through fasting, through watching, through generous love.*

Create in us a clean heart, O God;

And renew a right spirit within us.

God, whose glory it is always to have mercy; be gracious to all who have gone astray from your ways, and bring them again with penitent hearts and steadfast faith to embrace and hold fast the unchangeable truth of your Word, Jesus Christ our Lord. *ECUSA Book of Common Prayer*

34 God our Father, in your love and goodness you have taught us to overcome our sins with prayer, fasting and generosity; accept our Lenten disciplines, and when we fall by our weakness, raise us up by your unfailing mercy; through Jesus Christ our Lord.

David Silk

EASTER

35 *The life Christ lives, he lives to God, alleluia.*

Open me the gates of righteousness, alleluia;

And I will enter and give thanks to the Lord, alleluia.

God, who by the glorious resurrection of your Son destroyed death and brought life and immortality to light; grant that we, who have been raised with him, may abide in his presence and rejoice in the hope of eternal glory; through him who is our living Redeemer. *David Silk*

36 Almighty Father, who gave your Son to die for our sins and to rise again for our justification; grant that we who have been born again in union with him, may so put away the leaven of malice and wickedness, that we may always serve you in pureness of living and truth; through the same Christ our Lord.

*Book of Common Prayer**

ASCENSION

37 *God has gone up with the sound of rejoicing, and the Lord to the blast of the horn, alleluia.*

Sing praises, sing praises to God, alleluia;
Sing praises, sing praises to our King, alleluia.

God eternal, your Son the judge of the world and Lord of all has passed beyond our sight; may we so follow him in patient work and suffering that we may share his heavenly glory; through him who is our Mediator and Advocate.

38 God, whose Son our great High Priest has entered once for all into the holy place; by his intercession fulfil your gracious purpose and gather together in one all things in Christ who is head over all in the Church which is his body; through the same Christ our Lord.

PENTECOST

39 *The Spirit of the Lord fills the whole world; he holds all things together, and knows every word spoken by man, alleluia.*

Those who are led by the Spirit of God, alleluia;
They are the sons of God, alleluia.

Almighty God, on this day you opened the way to eternal life to every race and nation by the promised gift of your Holy Spirit; shed abroad this gift throughout the world by the preaching of the Gospel, that it may reach to the ends of the earth; through Jesus Christ our Lord.

ECUSA Book of Common Prayer

40 God, according to your promise you have given your Holy Spirit to us your people, that we might know the freedom of your children and taste on earth our heavenly inheritance; let us always maintain the unity he gives, and, living in his power, be your witnesses to all men; through Jesus Christ our Lord.

Church of South India

Sundays and other Holy Days

THE NINTH SUNDAY BEFORE CHRISTMAS

41 Creation

God eternal, in whom we live and move and have our being; awaken us to your presence that we may walk in your world as your children. Grant us reverence for all your creation, that we may treat our fellow men with courtesy, and all things living with gentleness; through Jesus Christ our Lord.

*New Every Morning**

42 God's world

Lord, you have taught us that the world is yours and those who dwell on it. Hear us therefore as we pray for the life of the world; that every nation may seek the way that leads to peace; that human rights and freedom may everywhere be respected; and that the earth's resources may be ungrudgingly shared among all men. We ask this through Jesus Christ our Lord.

A Christian's Prayer Book

43 Those in need

God of love, you see all the suffering, injustice and misery which reign in this world; have pity, we pray, on what you have created; in your mercy look upon the poor, the oppressed, the destitute, and all who are heavy-laden; fill our hearts with deep compassion for those who suffer, and hasten the coming of your kingdom of justice and truth; for the sake of Jesus Christ our Lord.

*Eugene Bersier**

THE EIGHTH SUNDAY BEFORE CHRISTMAS

44 The use of knowledge

Deliver us, O God, from following the fashions of the day in our thinking. Save us from the worship of power, whether power over nature or over men. Save us from the worship of science, and grant that, giving you thanks for the skill of the scientist, we may be preserved from the abuse of his discoveries. Help us never to confuse the creature with the Creator, or man with God. May we acknowledge man's reason as your gift, and, being freed from all false hopes and misplaced trust, find in you our hope and salvation; through Jesus Christ our Lord.

*Student Prayer**

45 The Church

Most gracious Father, we pray for your holy catholic Church. Fill it with all truth; in all truth with all peace. Where it is corrupt, purge it; where it is in error, direct it; where anything is amiss, reform it; where it is right, strengthen and confirm it; where it is in want, furnish it; where it is divided, heal it, and unite it in your love; through Jesus Christ our Lord.

*William Laud**

46 Social Workers

God, our heavenly Father, you know our needs and you care for us all. We pray for all who give support and counsel to their fellow men; for probation officers. . . and all other social workers; for all who by their skill and training ease the burden of the aged, the lonely and the perplexed, and guide those who have lost their way; that they may have both wisdom and sympathy, and see men through the eyes of Christ, who saw the crowd distressed and scattered as sheep without a shepherd; grant this for his sake, our Lord and Saviour.

*H. P. Leatherland**

THE SEVENTH SUNDAY BEFORE CHRISTMAS

47 Guidance

Lord God, you call your servants to ventures of which we cannot see the ending, by paths as yet untrodden, through perils unknown; give us faith to go out with good courage, not knowing whither we go, but only that your hand is leading us, and your love supporting us; to the glory of your name.

48 The Jews

O God, the God of Abraham, remember your everlasting covenant, and bring back your chosen people from exile. Open their hearts to your love and truth that, as they know you to be the only God, they may acknowledge Jesus whom you have sent to be our Messiah and Saviour. *David Silk*

49 The increase of the ministry

Raise up, O God, for the work of the ministry men of spiritual maturity and strong faith; men of wide vision and sound judgement; and above all men with a deep love for their Lord and for their fellows; that your Church may be served in days to come by those whose lives are wholly dedicated to the furtherance of your kingdom; through Jesus Christ our Lord. *Frank Colquhoun*

THE SIXTH SUNDAY BEFORE CHRISTMAS

50 Discipleship

Give us, Lord, the determination, which no unworthy affection can curb; give us the strength, which no tribulation can sap; give us the integrity, which no base purpose can seduce. Bestow on us also, Lord our God, understanding to know you, persistence to seek you, wisdom to find you, and a faithfulness which may at the end embrace you; through Jesus Christ our Lord. *Saint Thomas Aquinas*

51 Those in bondage

Our heavenly Father, we commend to your mercy those for whom life does not spell freedom: prisoners of conscience, the homeless and the handicapped, the sick in body and mind, the elderly who are confined to their homes, those who are enslaved by their passions, and those who are addicted to drugs. Grant that, whatever their outward circumstances, they may find inward freedom, through him who proclaimed release to captives, Jesus Christ our Saviour. *John R. W. Stott*

52 The homeless and refugees

O God, the Father of our Lord Jesus Christ, who in perfect love for man chose to live as one who had nowhere to lay his head; we pray for all who are homeless, all refugees, all who must live in exile or in a strange land; grant them human friendship in their need and loneliness, the chance of a new beginning, and the courage to take it, and, above all, an abiding faith in your sure love and care; through Jesus Christ our Lord. *Christian Aid*

THE FIFTH SUNDAY BEFORE CHRISTMAS

53 The Church

We pray you, Lord, to direct and guide your Church with your unfailing care, that it may be vigilant in times of quiet, and daring in times of trouble; through Jesus Christ our Lord. *Franciscan Breviary*

54 The Bible

Gracious God and most merciful Father, you have entrusted us with the rich and precious jewel of your holy word; inspire us with your Spirit that it may be written in our hearts to sustain us, to reform us, to renew us according to your own image, to build us into the perfect building of Christ, and to foster in us all heavenly virtues. Grant this prayer, Father, for the sake of Jesus Christ. *Geneva Bible**

55 Peace and justice

God of all nations, we pray you for all the people of your earth; for those who are consumed in mutual hatred and bitterness; for those who make war on their neighbours; for those who tyrannously oppress; for those who groan under cruelty and subjection.

We ask you to teach mankind to live together in peace, no man exploiting the weak, no man hating the strong, each race working out its own destiny, unfettered, self-respecting, fearless.

Teach us to be worthy of freedom, free from social wrong, free from individual oppression and contempt, pure of heart and hand, defrauding none, giving to all men – in all dealings of life – the honour we owe to those who are your children, whatever their colour, their race or their caste; through Jesus Christ our Lord. *J. S. Hoyland**

THE ADVENT WREATH

56 The Advent wreath has four blue (or sometimes red) candles in a ring around a white (or gold) one. The first candle is lit on Advent Sunday; additional ones are lit, one on each Sunday, and the white one on Christmas morning. On each occasion a suitable prayer may be said; if the themes of the Calendar and Lectionary are not used, the following traditional order may be observed:

Advent 1	The Prophets
Advent 2	John the Baptist
Advent 3	The Blessed Virgin Mary
Advent 4	God's People
Christmas Day	The Nativity

ADVENT SUNDAY

57 The coming of Christ

Keep us, O Lord, while we tarry on this earth, in a serious seeking after you, and in an affectionate walking with you, every day of our lives; that when you come, we may be found not hiding our talent, nor serving the flesh, nor yet asleep with our lamp unfurnished, but waiting and longing for our Lord, our glorious God for ever. *Richard Baxter**

58 Patience

O God, by whose command the order of time runs its course; forgive our impatience, perfect our faith, and, while we wait for the fulfilment of your promises, grant us to have a good hope because of your word; through Jesus Christ our Lord.

Gregory of Nazianzen

59 Just Judgement

O great and glorious God, holy and immortal, you search out the policies of nations and try the hearts of men; come, we pray, in judgement, upon the nations of the world; come, and bring to destruction all that is contrary to your holy will for mankind, and cause the counsels of the wicked to perish. Come, Lord, into our hearts, and root out from them all that you see, and we cannot see, to be unlike the Spirit of your Son, Jesus Christ our Lord.

*Harold Anson**

(See also 27 and 28)

ADVENT 2

60 The coming of Christ

O Lord our God, make us watchful and keep us faithful as we await the coming of your Son our Lord; that when he shall appear, he may not find us sleeping in sin, but active in his service and joyful in his praise, for the glory of your holy name.

Gelasian Sacramentary

61 The Bible

Grant, Lord, that we may love to read your holy word, in which is wisdom, in which is the royal law, in which are the living oracles of God; and may so read it that we may know and serve you better; through Jesus Christ our Lord.

After the Coronation Service

62 Those in need

God of love, whose compassion never fails; we bring to you the sufferings of all mankind; the needs of the homeless; the cry of prisoners; the pains of the sick and injured; the sorrow of the bereaved; the helplessness of the aged and weak. Strengthen and relieve them, Father, according to their various needs and your great mercy; for the sake of your Son our Saviour Jesus Christ. *After Saint Anselm*

ADVENT 3

63 Judgement

O Lord Christ, before whose judgement seat we must all appear; keep us stedfast and faithful in your service, and enable us so to judge ourselves in this life, that we may not be condemned in the day of your appearing; for your tender mercy's sake.

After William Bright

64 Industrial peace and national unity

God, the king of righteousness, lead us, we pray, in ways of justice and peace; inspire us to break down all tyranny and oppression, to gain for every man his due reward, and from every man his due service; that each may live for all, and all may care for each, in the name of Jesus Christ our Lord.

*William Temple**

65 The ordained ministry

Lord Jesus Christ, Apostle, Priest and Servant, bless the bishops, priests and deacons of your Church; may they lead your people boldly, walk with them lovingly, and send them forth joyfully to proclaim the good news of your kingdom where you live for ever and ever. *ACCM*

ADVENT 4

66 The Kingdom of God

O Lord, you have set before us the great hope that your kingdom shall come on earth, and have taught us to pray for its coming; give us grace to discern the signs of its dawning, and to work for the perfect day when your will shall be done on earth as it is in heaven; through Jesus Christ our Lord.

*Percy Dearmer**

67 Family life

God our Father, whose Son our Lord grew up in a home at Nazareth; we pray that family life may be hallowed by prayer and graced by love, joy and peace. Give to parents care and understanding in the training of their children; and may they, by their teaching and example, lead them in the way of Christ, that they may grow in grace and in the knowledge of your love; for the honour and glory of your name. *Adapted from Contemporary Parish Prayers*

68 Humility

Take from us, O God, all pride and vanity, all boasting and self-assertion, and give us the true courage that shows itself in gentleness, the true wisdom that shows itself in simplicity, and the true power that shows itself in modesty; through Jesus Christ our Lord. *Charles Kingsley**

69 The Advent Antiphons

O Wisdom, you come forth from the mouth of the Most High; you fill the universe and hold all things together with gentle strength: Come and teach us the way of truth.

Come, Lord Jesus.

O Adonai and Leader of Israel, you appeared to Moses in a burning bush and gave him the law on Sinai: Come and set us free with your mighty power.

Come, Lord Jesus.

O Stock of Jesse, you stand as an ensign for the nations; kings fall silent before you whom the nations long for: Come and deliver us without delay.

Come, Lord Jesus.

O Key of David and Sceptre of Israel, what you open no one can close, and what you close no one

can open: Come and deliver the captive from prison; free those who sit in darkness and in the shadow of death.
Come, Lord Jesus.
O Rising Sun, you are the splendour of eternal light and the sun of righteousness: Come and enlighten those who sit in darkness and in the shadow of death.
Come, Lord Jesus.
O King of the nations and their desire, you are the cornerstone which makes both one: Come and save man whom you formed from clay.
Come, Lord Jesus.
O Emmanuel, you are our King and our Judge, the one for whom the nations yearn and their Saviour: Come and save, our Lord and God.
Come, Lord Jesus. *Sarum Breviary*

CHRISTMAS

70 A Bidding Prayer

Dear friends in Christ, at this Christmas time let it be our care and delight to prepare ourselves to hear again the message of the angels, and in heart and mind to go to Bethlehem and see this thing that has happened, and the babe lying in a manger.
Therefore let us read and mark in Holy Scripture the story of the loving purposes of God from the first days of our disobedience until the glorious redemption brought us by this holy Child, and let us fill this place with the joy of our carols of praise.
But first let us pray for the needs of his whole world; for peace and goodwill over all the earth; for unity and brotherhood within the Church he came to build, and especially in the commonwealth of our sovereign lady Queen Elizabeth.

And because this of all things would gladden his heart, let us at this time remember in his name the poor and the helpless, the cold, the hungry, and the oppressed; the sick and those who mourn; the lonely and the unloved; the aged and the little children; all those who do not know the Lord Jesus, or who do not love him, or who by sin have grieved his heart of love.

Lastly let us remember before God all those who share our joy, but upon another shore and in a greater light, that vast throng which no one can count, whose hope was in the Word made flesh, and with whom, in this Lord Jesus, we for evermore are one.

These prayers and praises let us offer to our heavenly Father in the words which our Saviour Christ himself has taught us:

Our Father. . .

The almighty God bless us with his grace; Christ give us the joys of eternal life; and to the fellowship of the citizens above may the King of angels bring us all.

Adapted from Festival of Nine Lessons and Carols, King's College, Cambridge

71 A Bidding Prayer

In the name of Christ and his Church I bid you welcome to. . . (*Saint Nicholas'*) today. We have come together as the family of God in our Father's presence to prepare for (*or* celebrate) the festival of Christmas. In this service we hear and receive the story and message of the birth of Christ, and we offer to God our thanksgiving in the joyful singing of carols.

But first we pray:

For all christian people, that by this festival they may be renewed to fulfil Christ's work in the world;

For the world, which is already Christ's, that those who bear responsibility for its future, in politics, in industry, in commerce, in education, and in the mass media, may be inspired by the message of Christmas to work together for the establishment of justice, freedom and peace everywhere;
For all in special need, the sick, the anxious, the lonely, the fearful, and the bereaved.
We commend all whom we love, or who have asked for our prayers, to the unfailing love of our heavenly Father, and say together, as Christ himself taught us, *David Silk*
Our Father. . .
May the humility of the shepherds, the faith of the wise men, the joy of the angels, and the peace of the Christ Child, be God's gifts to us and to all men, this Christmas and always.

72 The Blessing of the Crib

In the name of the Father, and of the Son, and of the Holy Spirit.
Amen

BEFORE THE MIDNIGHT EUCHARIST

Today you will know that the Lord is coming to save us: and in the morning you will see his glory.

A reading from the Prophet Isaiah.

The Lord himself will give you a sign. It is this: the maiden is with child and will soon give birth to a son whom she will call Emmanuel, a name which means 'God-is-with-us.'

This is the word of the Lord.
Thanks be to God.

AFTER THE MIDNIGHT EUCHARIST

A light will shine on us this day: the Lord is born for us.

A reading from the Gospel according to Saint Luke.

When the angels had gone from them into heaven, the shepherds said one to another 'Let us go to Bethlehem and see this thing that has happened which the Lord has made known to us.' So they hurried away, and found Mary and Joseph, and the baby lying in a manger.

This is the word of the Lord.
Thanks be to God.
(Dear friends) let us pray that God our Father will bless this crib, and that all who worship his Son, born of the Virgin Mary, may come to share his life in glory.
God our Father, on this night (day) your Son Jesus Christ was born of the Virgin Mary for us men and for our salvation; bless + this crib which we have prepared to celebrate that holy birth; may all who see it be strengthened in faith, and receive the fullness of life he came to bring; who lives and reigns for ever and ever.
Amen.
The Lord bless us and keep us from all evil; and bring us to everlasting life.
Amen. *Church Literature Association*

73 Thanksgiving

To you, O Christ, Word of the Father, we offer our lowly praises and sincere thanks; For love of our fallen race you most wonderfully and humbly chose to be made man, and to take our nature as never more to lay it by; so that we might be born again by your Spirit and restored in the image of God; to whom, one blessed Trinity, be given all honour, might, majesty, and power, now and for ever.

*After the Third Collect**

74 The spirit of Christmas

God our Father, we ask that your son's birth as a little child may deliver us from the old slavery that holds us fast beneath the yoke of sin. Lord Jesus, by the example you gave in the poverty of your birth, teach us not to become so engrossed in material things that we lose sense of the true values of life. Spirit of love, inspire us with generosity towards people in misfortune and distress. We ask these prayers, giving glory to God in the highest, now and for evermore. *Catholic Prayer Book*

75 The Crib

Holy Jesus, to deliver us from the power of darkness you deigned to be born as man and laid in a manger; let the light of your love always shine in our hearts, and bring us at last to the joyful vision of your beauty, for you are now alive and reign with the Father and the Holy Spirit, God for ever and ever. *Parish Prayers**

76 Peace

O God, we thank you for the message of peace that Christmas brings to our distracted world. Give peace among the nations; peace in our land; peace in our homes; and peace in our hearts, as we remember the birth at Bethlehem of the Prince of peace, Jesus Christ our Lord. *Worship Now*

77 Peace

Sweet Child of Bethlehem, grant that we may share with all our hearts in this profound mystery of Christmas. Pour into the hearts of men the peace which they sometimes seek so desperately, and which you alone can give them. Help them to know one another better and to live as brothers, children of the same Father. Awaken in their hearts love and gratitude for your infinite goodness; join them together in your love; and give us all your heavenly peace. *Pope John XXIII*

78 Service

Father, we pray that the joy of Christmas may fill our hearts with a new and deeper sense of your love for us and for your world, and that we may reflect your love by serving those in need; for his sake, who came to be the Saviour of us all, Jesus Christ our Lord. *After William Bright*

79 Meditation before the Crib

i. The Word was made flesh
And dwelt among us

ii. Do I not fill heaven and earth? says the Lord.
Now he is made flesh and laid in a narrow manger.
From eternity to eternity you are God.
And now we see he is a child, a day old.

iii. We will praise you, Lord, because you gave Jesus Christ your Son to be born at this time of a pure Virgin.
We will praise you, Lord, because in the birth of your Son you have made a light to shine in our darkness.
We will praise you, Lord, because you choose to live among men, to be known as man.
True God of true God, Light of eternal Light, we adore you, Lord Christ, for you, though high in the glory of God the Father, did not abhor the womb of a Virgin, nor despise the nature of man.

iv. Welcome, all wonders in one sight!
Eternity shut in a span.
Summer in winter, Day in night,
  Heaven in earth, and God in man.

Great little one whose all-embracing birth
Brings earth to heaven, stoops heaven to earth.

v. Lord, by the song of the angels you made your birth known to shepherds, to your own people, and by the leading of the star to strangers. Teach us to know you now, and to make you known to all men.

vi. The kings, Lord, brought myrrh and frankincense and gold. Lord, we are nothing, we bring you what you have given, our lives for your life.

vii. Lord Jesus, Child of Mary, made man for the love of man, make in us a willing love for you and for our neighbours.

viii. Jesus, Son of David, Child of Mary, have mercy on us, and on all men.

Church Literature Association

(See also 25, 29 and 30)

CHRISTMAS 1

80 Peace

O God, our Father, who by the glorious birth of your Son gave new lustre to the world; let the light of his presence shine in the darkness of our lives, so that, filled with the spirit of his goodwill, the nations of the earth may inherit his gift of peace. We offer our prayer in his name.

81 The Presentation

Lord God, you kept faith with Simeon and showed him the infant King; give us grace to put all our trust in your promises, and the patience to wait a lifetime for their fulfilment; through Jesus Christ our Lord.

Susan Williams

82 Human need

Father in heaven, whose Son was made in the likeness of men to restore all men, to be the crown and model of human nature; grant life to the dead, health to the sick, and freedom to those in chains, that the life of mankind may be renewed in the knowledge and love of your Son Jesus Christ.

JANUARY 1

83 The Circumcision

Heavenly Father, whose blessed Son, that he might keep the law which he came to fulfil, received as on this day the outward circumcision; cleanse our minds by the inward circumcision from all incentives to sin, that we may worship you in spirit and in truth, in the same Christ Jesus, now and for evermore. *Parish Prayers**

84 The New Year

Grant, O Lord, that as the years change, we may find rest in your eternal changelessness. May we meet this new year bravely, sure in the faith that, while men come and go, and life changes around us, you are always the same, guiding us with your wisdom, and protecting us with your love; through our Saviour Jesus Christ. *William Temple**

85 The New Year

For all the possibilities ahead in this new year make us thankful, O Lord. Give us wisdom, courage, and discernment in the face of so much chaos, despair, and fear. Help us to see how, in our circumstances, we can contribute towards peace, faith and love. And give us the will to translate our desires into actions. *Brother John Charles, SSF*

86 The New Year

Lord Christ, Alpha and Omega, the beginning and the end, whose years never fail; may we so pass through the coming year with faithful hearts, that in all things we may please you and reflect your glory; for you are alive and reign with the Father and the Holy Spirit, one God, now and for ever.

Mozarabic Sacramentary

CHRISTMAS 2

87 The Holy Innocents

Heavenly Father, you saved your Son from Herod's anger and cruel designs; enable us to understand the plight of all who suffer undeservedly, and through us free the world from cruelty and oppression; for the sake of Jesus Christ our Lord.

Collects with the New Lectionary

88 Jesus in the temple

Lord Jesus Christ, who sat among the teachers both hearing them and asking them questions; give to us your people that humility of heart, and willingness to learn, without which no one can find wisdom; to the glory of your holy name. *Daily Prayer**

89 Guidance

O Lord, to be turned from you is to fall, to be turned to you is to rise, and to stand in you is to abide for ever; grant us in all our duties your help, in all our perplexities your guidance, in all our dangers your protection, and in all our sorrows your peace; through Jesus Christ our Lord. *Saint Augustine*

EPIPHANY

90 Thanksgiving

Praise be to you, O God, King of kings and Lord of lords; you alone are immortal and dwell in unapproachable light. No man has ever seen or can see you; yet you revealed yourself in Christ. He was manifested in human shape, attested by the Spirit, proclaimed among the nations, and believed in throughout the world. Through him creation is restored to unity, and mankind brought into your heavenly kingdom. To him be glory and power for ever. *I Timothy 6.16; 3.15*

91 The Star

Lord Jesus, our Master, go with us while we travel to the heavenly country; that, following your star, we may not wander in the darkness of this world's night, while you, who are our Way, and Truth, and Life, shine within us to our journey's end; for your mercy's sake. *Mozarabic Sacramentary*

92 Revelation

Eternal Wisdom, who made yourself known to the wise men as a child, in weakness not in power, in poverty not in wealth, as subject not as ruler; teach us to look for you where you are to be found, and bring us by your mercy to your eternal presence, for you are alive and reign with the Father and the Holy Spirit, God, now and for ever.

93 Mission

O God, who in the work of creation commanded the light to shine out of darkness; we pray that the light of the glorious gospel of Christ may shine into the hearts of all men everywhere, dispelling the darkness of ignorance and unbelief, and revealing to

them the knowledge of your glory in the face of Jesus Christ our Lord. *2 Corinthians 4.6*
(See also 31)

EPIPHANY 1

94 Increase of the ordained ministry
O Christ, our High Priest and Shepherd of souls; give to your Church Christlike pastors baptised with your Spirit, inspired by your truth, and filled with your love; for your own name's sake.
Ember Prayer

95 The Queen
Almighty God, our heavenly Father, bless Elizabeth our Queen. Help her to fulfil her responsibilities; that by her influence she may maintain unity, goodwill and peace among her peoples, and finally attain to the eternal kingdom of Christ; who is alive and reigns with you and the Holy Spirit, one God, now and for ever. *Service for the Silver Jubilee*

96 Volunteers for service overseas
God, whose Son Jesus Christ came to share our life on earth; hear our prayer for all who give voluntary service overseas, that in the spirit of Christ they may give of their best among those with whom they work and live; and through their service may the cause of peace in the world be strengthened; for the sake of our Lord Jesus Christ.
(See also 26, 32)

EPIPHANY 2

97 The increase of the ordained ministry
Almighty God, we praise you for those whom you

have called to the ministry of the Church from age to age. May those whom you would use today know your will; give them understanding of the task that awaits them; strengthen them as they prepare to fulfil your calling; and keep them humble and faithful in your service; for the glory of our Lord and Saviour Jesus Christ.

98 Leaders

We remember before you, O God, those who bear rule among us in Church and State, in industry and commerce; all who speak to us through broadcasting and the press; and all who have power over the lives of others. Grant them the humility to seek your guidance, and the courage to do your will, that our people may be led to the knowledge of you and to the service of your kingdom; through Jesus Christ our Lord.

99 The Sick

O God, the giver of life and health and joy, we pray that your will may be done in and for those who suffer sickness or disease. Through the ministry of men and women who have understanding and ability to help, may they be restored to soundness of body and mind; and through medical research and discovery may new cures be found to bring fresh hope to the world; through Jesus Christ our Lord.

EPIPHANY 3

100 Revelation

Gracious and holy Father, give us wisdom to perceive you, diligence to seek you, patience to wait for you, eyes to behold you, a heart to meditate on you, and a life to proclaim you; through the power of the Spirit of Jesus Christ our Lord. *Saint Benedict*

101 The underprivileged

O God our Father, in the name of him who gave bread to the hungry we remember all who, through our human ignorance, folly, selfishness and sin, are condemned to live in want; and we pray that all endeavours for the overcoming of world poverty and hunger may be so prospered that there may be found food sufficient for all. We ask this through Jesus Christ our Lord. *Christian Aid*

102 Alcoholics

O loving Saviour, in the mystery of the Eucharist you consecrate the fruit of the vine; give grace to all who degrade themselves by drinking to excess; and control and consecrate their lives to your service; through the merits of your fasting and temptation, and in union with the Father and the Holy Spirit.

*Henry Cooper**

EPIPHANY 4

103 Those in training for the ordained ministry

Help your servants, Lord, to be men of God, men of reconciliation, men of truth, men of prayer; and keep them humble in your service, for your mercy's sake. *ACCM*

104 Our country and people

Lord, bless this kingdom and commonwealth, that there may be peace and prosperity in all its borders. In peace so preserve it that it corrupt not; in trouble so defend it that it suffer not; and so order it, whether in plenty or in want, that it may faithfully serve you and patiently seek your kingdom, the only sure foundation both of men and states; through Jesus Christ our Saviour and Redeemer.

After William Laud

105 Artists and craftsmen

O God, whose Spirit in our hearts teaches us to desire your perfection, to seek for truth and to rejoice in beauty; enlighten and inspire all artists and craftsmen in whatever is true, pure and lovely, that your name may be honoured and your will done on earth; through Jesus Christ our Lord.

Society of Saint Luke the Painter

EPIPHANY 5

106 Revelation

Eternal Light, shine into our hearts; eternal Goodness, deliver us from evil; eternal Power, be our support; eternal Wisdom, scatter the darkness of our ignorance; eternal Pity, have mercy on us; that with all our heart and mind and strength we may seek your face and be brought by your infinite mercy to your holy presence; through Jesus Christ our Lord. *Alcuin*

107 Science

Lord, we have found out so much knowledge and yet possess so little wisdom. We pray that in your mercy you will save us from ourselves. Help us to learn the right use of nature no less quickly than we unlock her new treasures; and give us hearts and wills made new in Christ to dedicate your gifts of knowledge to the service of others and to the praise of your name. *Timothy Dudley-Smith*

108 Social Justice

O God, whose Son Jesus Christ cared for the welfare of everyone and went about doing good; grant us the imagination and perseverance to create in this country and throughout the world a just and loving society for the family of man; and make us agents of your compassion to the suffering, the persecuted and the oppressed, through the Spirit of your Son, who shared the sufferings of men, our pattern and our redeemer, Jesus Christ.

Norwich Cathedral

EPIPHANY 6

109 The Church

Grant, Lord, that we may hold to you without parting, worship you without wearying, serve you without failing; faithfully seek you, happily find you, and for ever possess you, the only God, blessed, now and for ever. *Saint Anselm*

110 Prison Staff

O Holy Spirit of God, inspire with your wisdom and love those with authority and responsibility in prisons; free them from contempt, hardness and carelessness, may they reflect that mercy and justice with which you rule and judge the hearts of men; through Jesus Christ our Saviour.

111 Stewardship of creation

God our Father, in whom we live and move and have our being, we thank you for the beauty of creation. May the achievements of men not disfigure it but enhance it to your greater glory.

We thank you for the wealth of the world's resources. May they not be squandered or wasted but shared justly among all people.

Accept our gratitude for all your bounty, and hear our prayer, for the sake of Jesus Christ our Lord.

Contemporary Parish Prayers

THE NINTH SUNDAY BEFORE EASTER

112 Knowledge

Almighty God, eternal, righteous and merciful, give us poor sinners to do for your sake all that we know of your will, and to will always what pleases you; that, inwardly purified, enlightened and kindled by the fire of your Holy Spirit, we may follow in the steps of your well-beloved Son, our Lord Jesus Christ.

Saint Francis of Assisi

113 Schools and Colleges

Almighty God, you are the source of truth, and your Spirit leads us into all truth; may all who teach and all who learn in our schools, colleges and universities be set free from everything that might hinder their search for the truth; and, finding truth, may they learn to use it for the good of mankind and for your greater glory. *James M. Todd*

114 The Use of Power

Almighty and eternal God, you have entrusted the minds of men with science and skill which can greatly bless or wholly destroy; grant us also a sense of responsibility and a stature of spirit to match your trust, that we may use our many inventions to your glory and the benefit of mankind; through Jesus Christ our Lord. *Peace Prayers 1946**

THE EIGHTH SUNDAY BEFORE EASTER

115 The Ministry of healing

O Lord and Master Jesus Christ, Word of the everlasting Father, you have borne our griefs and carried the burden of our weakness; renew by your

Spirit the gifts of healing in your Church, and send forth your disciples again to proclaim the good news of your kingdom, and to cure the sick and relieve your suffering children, to the praise and glory of your holy name. *Liturgy of Saint Mark*

116 Medical research

Almighty God, the Father of truth and understanding; give a clear vision to those who are engaged in medical research; grant them the spirit of patient discernment, that they may be skilled to find new ways of restoring health; and encourage them with the assurance that they are sharing your work; through Jesus Christ our Lord.

*F. B. Macnutt**

117 The sick

Lord Jesus Christ, in the days of your flesh the sick were brought to you for healing; hear us as we now bring to you in our prayers those who are ill, in body or mind; may your presence be with them to relieve suffering and distress, and to restore them to fulness of life; for your great love's sake.

Frank Colquhoun

THE SEVENTH SUNDAY BEFORE EASTER

118 Penitence

God, our Judge and Saviour, set before us the vision of your purity, and let us see our sins in the light of your holiness. Pierce our self-contentment with the shafts of your burning love, and let that love consume all that hinders us from perfect service of your cause; for as your holiness is our judgement, so are your wounds our salvation. *William Temple**

119 Social Services

We thank you, O God, for all who work in the social services: for policemen and probation officers; for youth leaders and school teachers; for welfare officers and psychiatric social workers; for doctors and nurses and many others. We pray that you will give to all such people sympathy and understanding, love and firmness, and the deeper knowledge that Jesus Christ is the only one who can make men truly whole. We ask this for his sake, our Saviour and our Lord. *Peter Markby*

120 Preparation of Lent

Lord Jesus, our Saviour, let us now come to you:
Our hearts are cold; Lord, warm them with your selfless love.
Our hearts are sinful; cleanse them with your precious blood.
Our hearts are weak; strengthen them with your joyous Spirit.
Our hearts are empty; fill them with your divine presence.
Lord Jesus, our hearts are yours; possess them always and only for yourself. *After Saint Augustine*

ASH WEDNESDAY

121 Lent

Almighty God, we pray that through this season of Lent, by prayer and study and self discipline, we may penetrate more deeply into the mystery of Christ's sufferings; that, following in the way of his cross and passion, we may come to share in the glory and triumph of his resurrection; through Jesus Christ our Lord. *Contemporary Parish Prayers*

122 Our Lenten rule

Save us, O God, from the false piety that parades itself in the eyes of men and is not genuine in your sight; and so inspire us by your Spirit that both in motive and deed, we may offer you acceptable service; through Christ our Lord. *Frank Colquhoun**

123 Penitence

Lord our God, grant us grace to desire you with our whole heart; that so desiring, we may seek and find you; and so finding, may love you; and so loving, may hate those sins from which you have delivered us; through Jesus Christ our Lord. *Saint Anselm*

124 The Blessing and Imposition of Ashes

If this order is used at the Eucharist, it follows the sermon, and the Creed and Prayers of Penitence may be omitted; if it is used at Morning or Evening Prayer, it follows the sermon, and the service may begin at: O Lord, open our lips: if it is used alone, it may be introduced by suitable readings and an address, and followed by prayers of intercession and dedication. The ashes are made by burning the palms of the previous year.

Almighty God, you have created us out of the dust of the earth; Grant that these ashes + may be to us a sign of our mortality and penitence, that we may remember that it is only by your gracious gift that we are given everlasting life; through Jesus Christ our Saviour.

Amen.

The priest first signs himself, and then those who come forward to the rail, with these words:

+ Remember that you are dust, and to dust you shall return. *ECUSA, The Book of Common Prayer.*

Suitable hymns or psalms may be sung during the imposition. The priest then washes his hands, or cleans them with breadcrumbs, and the eucharist continues with the Intercession and the Peace. The remaining ashes should be placed on clean earth after the service.

LENT 1

125 The Bible

Enable us, our Father, to respond to the grace of your word with humility of heart and in the spirit of loving obedience; that our wills may be brought into submission to your perfect will, and our lives be conformed more and more to the image of your Son, Jesus Christ our Lord.

Contemporary Parish Prayers

126 Those in need

Almighty and everlasting God, the comfort of the sad, the strength of those who suffer; hear the prayers of your children who cry out of any trouble; and to every distressed soul grant mercy, relief and refreshment; through Jesus Christ our Lord.

Gelasian Sacramentary

127 The European Community

Lord, we ask you to guide and direct the members of the European Community; draw us closer to each other, and help us to attain justice and freedom, and to use our resources for the good of all mankind; through Jesus Christ our Lord.

Revised Services of the Church of Ireland

LENT 2

128 Body and mind

Eternal God, you have made all things for man, and man for your glory; sanctify our bodies and souls, our thoughts and our intentions, our words and our actions. Let our body be a servant of our mind, and both body and spirit servants of Jesus Christ; that doing all things for your glory here, we may share your glory hereafter; through the same Jesus Christ our Lord. *Jeremy Taylor**

129 The ordained ministry

O God, you make your messengers winds and your ministers flames of fire; stir up and strengthen the sacred gift of orders in all stewards of your mysteries, that they may gather out of your kingdom everything which prevents its growth, and may kindle in the hearts of all that fire which you came to send on earth; to the glory of your name.

*Henry P. Liddon**

130 The mentally ill

Father, we pray for the mentally ill, for all who are of a disturbed and troubled mind. Be to them light in their darkness, their refuge and strength in time of fear. Give special skills and tender hearts to all who care for them, and show them how best to assist in your work of healing; through Jesus Christ our Lord. *Timothy Dudley-Smith*

LENT 3

131 Retaliation

God our Father, whose strong Son made no answer to insult and false accusation; strengthen us to follow the pattern of his life and death, and, in the face of injustice, to trust ourselves to you, our faithful Creator and righteous Judge; for his name's sake.

132 Racial Harmony

God of peace, look in mercy upon the sons of men, and increase the spirit of sympathy and understanding between those of different race and colour.

Strengthen the love of justice and liberty among all peoples, and bring the whole earth to acknowledge your sovereignty of love and truth; through Jesus Christ our Lord.

133 Those in need

Lord Jesus, by the loneliness of your suffering on the cross, be near to all who are desolate, and in pain and sorrow; and let your presence transform their sorrow into comfort, and their loneliness into fellowship with you; for the sake of your tender mercy. *Sursum Corda**

LENT 4

134 Lent

Heavenly Father, give us more charity, more self-denial, more likeness to Christ. Teach us that it is better to give than to receive; better to forget ourselves than to put ourselves forward; better to serve than to be served, after the example of your Son, Jesus Christ our Lord. *Henry Alford**

135 Religious Communities

O Lord, who for our sake became poor, that we through your poverty might become rich; strengthen all those who, at your call and after your example, have left possessions, parents, hope of family, and their own wills, that they might take up the cross and follow you in the threefold way of poverty, chastity and obedience. Through the consecration of their lives and the power of their prayers may your Church be strengthened to be the more perfectly conformed to your image; for you are alive and reign with the Father and the Spirit, one God, now and for ever. *South African Prayer Book*

136 The Queen

O Lord our Governor, we pray for your servant Elizabeth, set over us in your providence to be our Queen. Give her grace and wisdom to fulfil the varied duties of her calling, enrich her in the life of her family and her home; and may she always be a source of strength and inspiration to her people, and promote your honour and glory; through Jesus Christ our Lord. *Frank Colquhoun*

LENT 5

137 Mission

O God of all the nations of the earth, remember those who, though created in your image, are ignorant of your love; and, in fulfilment of the sacrifice of your Son Jesus Christ, let the prayers and labours of your Church deliver them from false faith and unbelief, and bring them to worship you; through him who is the resurrection and the life of all who put their trust in you, Jesus Christ our Lord.

Saint Francis Xavier

138 Peace

O God, whose will is to fold both heaven and earth in a single peace; let the design of your great love lighten upon the waste of our wraths and sorrows; and give peace to your Church, peace among nations, peace in our homes, and peace in our hearts; through your Son our Saviour Jesus Christ.

*After the Third Collect**

139 Drug Addicts

Almighty Father, whose blessed Son refused at Calvary the deadening wine; have pity on all who seek unlawful escape from their sorrows, and by the virtue of his cross give them grace to share his passion and his victory, who with the Comforter and you reigns triumphant in eternal joy.

Henry Cooper

PALM SUNDAY

140 The Blessing and Procession of Palms

The congregation assembles in a place apart from the church where the Liturgy is to be celebrated. The palms may be distributed to them before the service begins, or after they have been blessed. This antiphon, or a hymn, is used as the ministers enter:

i Hosanna to the Son of David! Blessings on him who comes in the name of the Lord! Hosanna in the highest!

ii After the greeting the priest may give a brief explanation: he then blesses the palms:

Almighty God, whose Son Jesus Christ was greeted on this day as King; grant that as we now honour him by carrying these branches + *of palm,* so we may always seek your glory by obedience to your will; through the same Jesus Christ our Lord.

Amen.

The account of the Lord's entrance into Jerusalem is read from one of the Gospels: Matthew 21. 1–9 or Mark 11. 1–10 or Luke 19. 29-38, and the usual responses are said.

The procession to the church:

iii Let us go forth in peace, praising Jesus our Messiah. *Joint Liturgical Group*

The Eucharist begins at the collect for the day, the Passion is read for the Gospel, and the Prayers of Penitence and the Creed may be omitted; Morning and Evening Prayer begin at 'O Lord, open our lips'; if this ceremony takes place apart from another service, a suitable order is:

Readings: Zechariah 9. 9–12. Psalm 45. 1–8. 1 Corinthians 1. 18–25.
Gospel: as above
Address:
Prayers of Intercession and Penitence
The Blessing of Palms
Procession
Prayer of Dedication.

141 Charity

Lord, save us from being self-centred in our prayers and teach us to remember to pray for others. May we be so bound up in love with those for whom we pray, that we may feel their needs as acutely as our own, and intercede for them with sensitivity, with understanding and with imagination. We ask this in Christ's name. *After John Calvin*

142 The ordained ministry

Grant, O God, that the same mind may be in all the ministers of your Church which was in Christ Jesus: his self-forgetting humility, his interest in common things, his love for common people, his compassion for the fallen, his tolerance with the mistaken, his patience with the slow; and in all their work and ministry make them continually sensitive to your guidance and ready to do your will; through Jesus Christ our Lord *Methodist Book of Offices**

143 Those in need

Lord God, our heavenly Father, regard, we pray, with your divine pity the pains of all your children; and grant that the passion of our Lord and his infinite love may make fruitful for good the tribulations of the innocent, the sufferings of the sick, and the sorrows of the bereaved; through him who suffered in our flesh and died for our sake, the same your Son our Saviour Jesus Christ.

MAUNDY THURSDAY

144 The Betrayal

God, our heavenly Father, who to redeem the world delivered up your only Son to be betrayed by one of his disciples and sold to his enemies; take from us, we pray, all greed and hypocrisy; and so strengthen us that, loving you above all things, we may remain steadfast in our faith to the end; through him who gave his life for us, our Saviour Jesus Christ.

L. Tuttiet

145 The Washing of Feet

If the Washing of Feet takes place at the Eucharist, it follows the sermon, and the Creed and Prayers of Penitence are omitted.

Lord Jesus Christ, who when about to institute your holy Sacrament at the Last Supper washed the feet of the apostles, and taught us by your example the grace of humility; cleanse us, we pray, from all stain of sin, that we may be prepared to share your holy mysteries; for you are alive and reign with the Father and the Holy Spirit, one God, now and for ever. *The Royal Maundy**

146 The Unity of the Church

Lord Jesus Christ, you said to your apostles:
I leave you peace, my peace I give you.
Look not on our sins but on the faith of your Church,
and grant us the peace and unity of your kingdom
where you live for ever and ever. *ICEL*

147 The Denial

O Lord Jesus Christ, look upon us with those eyes of yours, the eyes with which you looked upon Peter in the hall of judgement, that with Peter we may repent, and by your great love be forgiven and restored; for your mercy's sake. *Lancelot Andrewes**

(see also 20 and 21)

GOOD FRIDAY

By a long and widespread tradition there is usually no celebration of the Eucharist on Good Friday, although Holy Communion is sometimes received from the bread (and wine) consecrated on Maundy Thursday. The Intercession of Ante-communion may be followed by a procession of the cross, the Reproaches, or other suitable hymns, silent adoration, the Lord's Prayer, and the distribution of Holy Communion. If it is desired to extend the service to fill the period between 12 noon and 3 o'clock, Morning and Evening Prayer, the Litany, and Meditation on the Seven Words are all appropriate.

At the Stations of the Cross, or during the meditations on the Seven Words, the following responses may be used to introduce or conclude each section:

148 We adore you, Christ, and we bless you;
Because by your holy cross you have redeemed the world.

149 Saviour of the world, you have redeemed us by your passion and cross.
Save us, and help us, we humbly pray.

150 The Way of the Cross

Lord Christ, who entered into your triumph by the hard and lonely way of the cross; may your courage and loyalty, and your unswerving devotion to the Father's will, inspire and strengthen us to tread firmly and with joy the road which love bids us take, even though it may lead us through suffering, misunderstanding and darkness. We ask this for your sake, who, for the joy that was set before you, endured the cross, despising the shame, and are now seated at the right hand of the throne of God the Father.

*With all our strength**

151 Jesus is condemned to death

O Lord Jesus Christ, whose unjust judgement we justly condemn; save us from all malice and uncharitableness in accusing our brethren, lest what we do unto others we do unto you, and doom you afresh, our Saviour and God for ever and ever.

*A Procession of Passion Prayers**

152 **Jesus bears his cross**
Blessed Lord, for our sake you were content to bear the cross of sorrow, want and death; fill us with your spirit of self-sacrifice and love, that we may complete your suffering by sharing the burdens of all who need our help and care.

153 **Jesus falls**
You know, Lord, how often we have to walk the tightrope between truth and goodwill, between one principle and another, between one view and another, between one person and another; let us ever keep our eyes on your truth, and so walk without stumbling; when we slip, support us with your love; through Christ our Lord.

154 Almighty God, who gave your only Son to die for the sins of the world; have mercy on all who are tempted and on all who through weakness or wilfulness fall into sin; reveal to them your gracious love, that, turning to you for help, they may be led into fellowship with you and obedience to your will; through Jesus Christ our Lord.

155 God, the Father of our Lord Jesus Christ, who in perfect love for man chose the way of rejection and death; remember all who must live in exile or a strange land, all who are cut off from their fellow men; support them in their loneliness and need, grant them the vision of a new beginning and the courage to take it, and, through the warmth of human friendship, strengthen their faith in your love and care; through Christ our Lord.

156 **Jesus and his Mother**
Lord Christ, in whose passion was fulfilled the prophecy of Simeon to Mary; give us her courage

and faith to open ourselves to the truth however it may hurt and disturb us, for thus we share your way of sorrow and joy. *David Silk*

157 Jesus is helped

Heavenly Father, your love embraces all nations on earth; free us from racial prejudice and the denial of human dignity; and, by the cross which Simon carried, draw together in one true fellowship men of all races and languages, that justice, mercy and peace may be established everywhere; through Jesus Christ our Lord.

158 O Lord Jesus Christ, whose Cross has painted bright your love; imprint on our hearts the love with which you have loved us; that we may display your likeness along all our paths, unto all for whom you have died; for you are alive and reign in the glory of the eternal Trinity, God for ever and ever.

*A Procession of Passion Prayers**

159 The Women of Jerusalem

Lord God, as we your sons and daughters look upon the Saviour for our sake ready to die, may we mourn not for him, whose pains were our glory, but for ourselves, whose shames are his wounds; and repent unto you, who with the same your Son and the Holy Spirit are one God, holy and pitiful, for ever and ever. *Adapted from E. Milner-White*

160 The Gate of the City

O Lord Jesus Christ, Son of the living God, who would not enter your own heaven but through the strait gate of scorning and wounds; where you have gone before, let us not fear to follow, nor turn for any pain out of the way that leads to you; for you are alive and reign with the Father and the Holy Spirit, one God, world without end.

*A Procession of Passion Prayers**

161 The Crucifixion

O Lord and Saviour, stripped naked upon your Cross, yet robed eternally in holiness and light; take from us the rags both of our sins and our imagined righteousnesses; and clothe us with the mantle of your praise in Sion; where you are alive and reign in the glory of the Father and the Holy Spirit, ever one God, world without end.

*A Procession of Passion Prayers**

162 O Lord, our Saviour and our God, whom nails could not hold to the Cross, but only love; grant that we, who have received the fulness of your love, may be ready to bear before the world the marks of your Passion; for you are alive and reign with the Father and the Holy Spirit, one God, world without end.

*A Procession of Passion Prayers**

163 O Christ, the Master Carpenter of Nazareth, on a cross through wood and nails you have wrought man's salvation; wield well your tools in the workshop of your world, so that we, who come to you rough-hewn, may by you be fashioned according to your will; for the sake of your tender mercy.

*C.I.T.C. Schools Prayer, Nairobi**

164 The Seven Words

O Lord Jesus Christ, who from out your silence upon the Cross did bequeath to your Church Seven Words; grant that we may ponder them as the inexhaustible Gospel of your love and of the world's redemption; and learn likewise both by speech and silence to glorify our Father in heaven; who with you and the

Holy Spirit is alive and reigns, one God, world without end. *A Procession of Passion Prayers**

165 'Father, forgive them' *Luke 23.34*
Grant us, O Lord, the glory of praying with our Master, the Crucified, by praying for our enemies, and forgiving those who wrong or despitefully use us; that we ourselves may better deserve the gift of your glorious pardon; through the same Jesus Christ our Lord. *A Procession of Passion Prayers**

166 'Today you will be with me in Paradise' *Luke 23.43*
Help us, Lord, to see ourselves as you see us, and, in shame for what we are, to cast ourselves in trust upon your love; speak to us the word of pardon, for our trust is not in any virtue or wisdom of our own, but only in the mercy and love of God, which you have shown us in your life and death, our Lord and our God. *William Temple**

167 'Here is your mother' *John 19.26–27*
O Lord Jesus Christ, Son of the living God, whose love, streaming from the bare Cross, entrusted your best beloved, mother and disciple, each to the other; bestow on us the grace and glory of forgetting ourselves in a constant tender healing of the sorrows of those whom you love; for your mercy's sake.
Adapted from E. Milner-White

168 'My God, why have you forsaken me?'
Matthew 27. 46
Lord Jesus Christ, who for us endured the horror of deep darkness; teach us by the depth of your agony the vileness of our sin, and so bind us to yourself in bonds of gratitude and love, that we may be united with you in your perfect sacrifice, our Saviour, our Lord and our God. *William Temple**

169 'I thirst' *John 19.28*

Lord Jesus Christ, Son of the living God, who at the sixth hour with great turmoil went up to the cross of pain on Golgotha, and, thirsting for our salvation, accepted the full sponge of vinegar; kindle in our hearts the burning love of your passion, and let us continually find our delight in you alone, our crucified Lord. *Sext*

170 'It is accomplished' *John 19.30*

Lord God, when you call your servants to endeavour any great matter, grant us also to know that it is not the beginning, but the continuing of the same, until it be thoroughly finished, which yields the true glory; through him who, for the finishing of your work, laid down his life for us, our Redeemer, Jesus Christ. *After Sir Francis Drake*

171 'Into your hands I commend my spirit' *Luke 23.46*

Lord Jesus Christ, Son of the living God, who at the ninth hour, with outstretched hands and bowed head commended your spirit to God the Father, and by your death unlocked the gates of paradise; grant that in the hour of our death we may come to you, the true paradise, for ever and ever. *None*

172 The Death of Christ

Blessed be your Name, O Jesu, Son of the most high God; blessed be the sorrow you suffered when your holy hands and feet were nailed to the tree; and blessed your love when, the fulness of pain accomplished, you gave your soul into the hands of the Father; so by your Cross and precious Blood redeeming all the world, all longing souls departed and the numberless unborn; for you are now alive and reign in the glory of the eternal Trinity, God for ever and ever.

*A Procession of Passion Prayers**

173 The Burial

Lord, as your loyal mourners lifted your torn body from the tree, and gently swathed it for repose; so let us faithfully go forth to bind up the wounded spirit and salve the broken life; in your dear Name, and to your sole praise, for you reign in the glory of the eternal Trinity, world without end.

*A Procession of Passion Prayers**

174 Welcome, Lord, into your calm and peaceful kingdom those who, out of this present life, have departed to be with you; grant them rest and a place with the spirits of the just; and give them the life that knows not age, the reward that passes not away; through Jesus Christ our Lord.

Saint Ignatius Loyola

175 Thanksgiving

Thanks be to God, who gives us the victory through our Lord Jesus Christ.

We praise you, Lord Jesus Christ, Son of God, for you submitted to the discipline of a son's obedience, and perfectly revealed in your death the loving nature of the Father.

We praise you, Lord Jesus Christ, Son of Man, for as champion of man and for his sake, you entered the battle against evil, and won the perfect victory over its power.

We praise you, Lord Jesus Christ, Servant of God, for you accepted the suffering of those who seek to be at one with those they serve, and by your sacrifice made us one with God.

Thanks be to God, who gives us the victory through our Lord Jesus Christ.

176 Litany for a Good Death

Suitable for Good Friday evening.

God the Father
have mercy on us.
God the Son
have mercy on us.
God the Holy Spirit
have mercy on us.
Holy, blessed, and glorious Trinity
have mercy on us.

God, who took the form of a servant, and shared the life of suffering and sorrow,
have mercy on us.
God, who raised the daughter of Jairus, the son of the widow of Nain, and Lazarus at Bethany,
have mercy on us.
God, who bore our weaknesses and healed our sicknesses,
have mercy on us.
God, who became obedient unto death, even death on a cross,
have mercy on us.
God, who at the beginning breathed life into man, and appointed the hour of our death,
have mercy on us.

Hear our prayers, good Jesus, and grant that, dying to sin here, we may live for you in heaven:
Good Jesus, hear us.
May we, remaining your faithful soldiers and servants here, receive hereafter the crown of glory:
Good Jesus, hear us.
May we accept with joy all the suffering of sickness and death as no more than we deserve:

Good Jesus, hear us.
Be with us in the valley of the shadow of death:
Good Jesus, hear us.
Let us not, at our last hour, fall away from you:
Good Jesus, hear us.
Forgive us our sins, and strengthen us with the Bread of Life:
Good Jesus, hear us.
Let us die in your faith and fear, in sure and certain hope of the resurrection to eternal life:
Good Jesus, hear us.
Deliver us, Lord, at our last hour: as you delivered Enoch and Elijah from the death which must come to all,
So save and deliver us.
As you delivered Noah from the flood,
So save and deliver us.
As you delivered Job from his affliction,
So save and deliver us.
As you delivered Isaac from the knife,
So save and deliver us.
As you delivered Lot from Sodom,
So save and deliver us.
As you delivered the children of Israel from Pharoah,
So save and deliver us.
As you delivered Daniel from the lions' den,
So save and deliver us.
As you delivered the three young men from the fiery furnace,
So save and deliver us.
As you have always delivered from evil those who put their trust in you,
So save and deliver us.

Deliver us, Lord, on that fearful day, when the heavens and the earth shall pass away, when you

shall come to judge the world by fire:
Save and deliver us.
In the day of judgement, when the books are opened, and the dead, great and small, shall stand before you:
Save and deliver us.
Holy God, holy and strong, holy and immortal:
Have mercy on us.
Jesus, Lamb of God:
Have mercy on us.
Jesus, bearer of our sins:
Have mercy on us.
Jesus, redeemer of the world:
Give us your peace.

Our Father in heaven,
hallowed be your Name,
your kingdom come,
your will be done,
on earth as in heaven.
Give us today our daily bread.
Forgive us our sins
as we forgive those who sin against us.
Lead us not into temptation
but deliver us from evil.

For the kingdom, the power, and the glory
are yours
now and for ever. Amen.

Happy are the dead:
Who die in the faith of Christ.

177 **i** Father, you made us in your image and your Son accepted death for our salvation. Help us to keep watch in prayer at all times. May we be free from sin when we leave this world, and rejoice in

peace with you for ever; through Jesus Christ our Lord.
Amen.

ii May the Lord of his mercy grant us, with all his faithful servants, eternal rest and peace.
Amen. *The Priest's Book of Private Devotion*

EASTER EVE

The liturgy begins after nightfall, and ends before daybreak on Easter Day.

The Service of Light

The church is in complete darkness, and a large fire is lit outside. The congregation, each with an unlit candle, may assemble near the fire; the priest greets them and introduces the service briefly. The lighted fire is blessed:

178 Almighty God, you sent your Son to be the light of the world and to bring to your people the radiance of your glory. Bless + this fire, and set us aflame with the fire of your love, that with pure hearts and minds we may come to the feast of everlasting light; through Jesus Christ our Lord.

179 The candle may be marked with the cross, the letters Alpha and Omega, and the numerals of the year:

Christ yesterday and today,
the beginning and the end,
Alpha and Omega;
his are all times
and all ages;
to him be glory and power
through all eternity.
Amen.

180 Five grains of incense may be inserted into the candle in the form of the cross:

By his holy
and glorious wounds
may the Lord Christ
guard us
and keep us.
Amen.

181 The candle is lit from the new fire:

May the light of Christ, rising in glory, dispel all the darkness of our hearts and minds.

182 The deacon takes the candle, lifts it high, and sings:

Christ our light!
Thanks be to God!

The priest's candle is lighted.

The deacon, carrying the Paschal Candle, leads the priest and people through the Church door. Inside he stops and raises the candle; and the versicle and response is repeated; the candles of the choir and servers are lit. The procession moves through the church to the chancel steps, where the deacon again stops, turns to the people, and raises the candle again; the versicle and response is said the third time; the candles of the congregation are lighted. The Paschal Candle is then placed in a prominent position, either in the sanctuary, or in the chancel, or near the pulpit, and the church lights are put on.

The Easter Proclamation is said:

183 Rejoice, heavenly powers! Sing, choirs of angels!
Exult, all creation around God's throne!
Jesus Christ, our King, is risen!
Sound the trumpet of salvation!

Rejoice, O earth, in shining splendour,
radiant in the brightness of your King!
Christ has conquered! Glory fills you!
Darkness vanishes for ever!

Rejoice, O Mother Church! Exult in glory!
The risen Saviour shines upon you!
Let this place resound with joy,
echoing the mighty song of all God's people!

The Lord be with you:
and also with you.
Lift up you hearts:
we lift them to the Lord.
Let us give thanks to the Lord our God:
It is right to give him thanks and praise.

It is truly right that with full hearts and minds and voices we should praise the unseen God, the all-powerful Father, and his only Son, our Lord Jesus Christ, who has ransomed us with his blood, and reconciled us to the Father!
This is our Passover feast, when Christ, the true Lamb, is slain, whose blood consecrates the homes of all believers.
This is the night when first you saved our fathers: you freed the people of Israel from their slavery and led them dry-shod through the sea.
This is the night when the pillar of fire destroyed the darkness of sin!
This is the night when Christians everywhere, washed clean of sin and freed from all defilement, are restored to grace and grow together in holiness.
This is the night when Jesus Christ broke the chains of death and rose triumphant from the grave.
What good would life have been to us, had Christ not come as our Redeemer?
Father, how wonderful your care for us! How boundless your merciful love!
To ransom a slave you gave away your Son.
O happy fault, O necessary sin of Adam, which gained for us so great a Redeemer!
Most blessed of all nights, chosen by God to see Christ rising from the dead!

Of this night Scripture says: 'The night will be as clear as day: it will become my light, my joy.'
The power of this holy night dispels all evil, washes guilt away, restores lost innocence, bring mourners joy; it casts out hatred, brings us peace, and humbles earthly pride.
Night truly blessed when heaven is wedded to earth and man is reconciled with God!
Therefore, heavenly Father, in the joy of this night, receive our evening sacrifice of praise, your Church's solemn offering.
Accept this Easter candle, a flame divided but undimmed, a pillar of fire that glows to the honour of God.
Let it mingle with the lights of heaven and continue bravely burning to dispel the darkness of this night!
May the Morning Star which never sets find this flame still burning, Christ, that Morning Star, who came back from the dead, and shed his peaceful light on all mankind, your Son who lives and reigns for ever and ever. Amen.

Joint Liturgical Group

The Ministry of the Word

The readings are introduced in these, or similar words:

(Dear friends in Christ,) we have begun our solemn vigil. Let us now listen attentively to the word of God, recalling how he saved his people throughout history and, in the fullness of time, sent his own Son to be our Redeemer. Through this Easter celebration, may God bring to perfection the saving work he has begun in us.

The readings follow. The account of the Exodus and the last two readings (Romans 6. 3–11 and The Gospel) are always used, but the others may be omitted. Each reading is followed by a psalm or canticle, or by silence; then follows the prayer.

i Genesis 1. 1, 26–31
Psalm 104. 1–6, 30
Collect for the Ninth Sunday before Christmas

ii Genesis 22. 1–2, 9–13, 15–18
Psalm 16. 1, 9–12
Collect for the Seventh Sunday before Christmas

iii Exodus 14. 15–15. 1
Exodus 15. 1–6
Collect for the Sixth Sunday before Christmas

iv Isaiah 54. 5–14
Psalm 30. 1–5. 12, 13
Prayer from Baptism, Confirmation, and Holy Communion (34)

v Isaiah 55. 1–11
Isaiah 12. 2–6
Collect for the Sunday before Advent (1)

vi Baruch 3. 9–15, 32–4. 4
Psalm 19. 7–10
Prayer from Baptism, Confirmation, and Holy Communion (35)

vii Ezekiel 36. 16–28
Psalm 42. 1–5; 43. 3, 4
Collect from Baptism, Confirmation, and Holy Communion (4)

The altar candles are lighted, and the Gloria is sung. Then is said the collect either for Easter Eve or Easter Day (1).

Reading: Romans 6. 3–11
Canticle or hymn. Psalm 118. 16–23 is suitable
Gospel: Matthew 28. 1–10 or Mark 16. 1–8 or Luke 24. 1–12
Sermon

The Renewal of Baptismal Promises

During the procession to the Font the Litany in the Alternative Service Book may be sung, or the following may be used:

184 Let us pray the all-holy and ever-blessed Trinity to send mercy and grace upon us and upon all people.
God the Father, have mercy on us:
God the Father, have mercy on us.
God the Son, have mercy on us:
God the Son, have mercy on us.
God the Holy Spirit, have mercy on us:
God the Holy Spirit, have mercy on us.
Stretch out your hand upon us. Lord, and save us; raise us up and defend us:
Lord, have mercy.
Let us pray for the peace which comes from above, and for the salvation of our souls:
Lord, have mercy.
Let us pray for the peace of the whole world, and for the welfare and unity of the Church of God:
Lord, have mercy.
Let us pray for the conversion of those in unbelief and error:
Lord, have mercy.
Let us pray for our country, for this place (or city), for this diocese, and for all who live there:
Lord, have mercy.
Let us pray for all Christian people throughout the world:
Lord, have mercy.
Let us pray for all Christian princes and governors, especially our sovereign lady, Queen Elizabeth:
Lord, have mercy.
Let us pray for all in authority in this land, especially those in this county (*or* city, *or* place):
Lord, have mercy.
Let us pray for the bishops and clergy of Christ's Church, especially for N, our bishop:
Lord, have mercy.
Let us pray for all voyagers and travellers:
Lord, have mercy.

Let us pray for stedfastness in the faith for our brothers and sisters beyond the seas:
Lord, have mercy.
Let us pray for all who are sick or suffering, in mind, or body:
Lord, have mercy.
Let us pray for a holy and happy death, for rest in paradise, and for the perfect vision of the glory of God:
Lord, have mercy.
Let us pray that we may follow the blessed saints and martyrs in bearing our cross before the world:
Lord, have mercy.
Let us pray for the faithful departed:
Lord, have mercy.

Holy Communion, Alternative Services, Series Two, originally in 1929 Prayer Book of the Scottish Episcopal Church

Then follows the blessing of the Water and the Renewal of Vows, unless the full rite of Baptism and Confirmation are to be celebrated.
The Eucharist continues at the Peace.

The Easter candle remains in its place until Pentecost, and is lit at every Baptism and Eucharist; it may also be lit at sung Morning and Evening Prayer.
After Pentecost it is removed to a place near the font, and is lit for Baptism. It may also be used at Funerals.

EASTER DAY

185 The Blessing of the Easter Garden

In the name of the Father, and of the Son, and of the Holy Spirit. *Amen.*

BEFORE THE EASTER VIGIL
Today you will know that the Lord is coming to save us: and in the morning you will see his glory.

A reading from the Prophet Hosea.

After two days the Lord will revive us; on the third day he will raise us up, that we may live before him. His going forth is sure as the dawn.
This is the word of the Lord.

AFTER THE EASTER VIGIL
The Lord has indeed risen, alleluia! Glory and kingship be his for ever and ever.

A reading from Saint Matthew's Gospel.

The angel said to the women, 'Do not be afraid; for I know that you seek Jesus who was crucified. He is not here; for he has risen as he said.'
This is the word of the Lord.
Thanks be to God.
(Dear friends) let us pray that God our Father will bless this Garden, and that all who worship his Son, risen from the dead, may come to share his unending life.

God our Father, on this night (or day) your Son Jesus Christ was raised from the dead in accordance with the Scriptures.
Bless + this Garden which we have prepared to celebrate his victory.
May all who see it be strengthened in faith, know the power of his presence, and rejoice in hope of eternal glory; for he is alive and reigns for ever and ever. *Amen.* *David Silk*
The Lord bless us and preserve us from all evil: and keep us in life eternal. *Amen.*

186 Prayers at the Easter Garden

i Christ is risen from the dead, alleluia!
He is risen indeed, alleluia!

ii See, I am doing a new thing, says the Lord. Now it comes to light; can you not see it? I am making the whole of creation new.

iii We praise you, Christ, for you are the First and the Last, and the Living One.
We praise you, Christ, for you died; and, behold, you are alive for evermore; you have the keys of Death and Hades.
We praise you, Christ, for you are now our unseen companion along the daily journey of life.
We praise you, Christ, for you took to yourself our humanity, and carried it into life eternal.

iv God our Father, may the whole world join in a hymn of thanksgiving for the great love you have shown us in Jesus Christ our Lord, risen from the dead, and may our hearts and lives echo your praise, now and for ever.

v Risen Lord Jesus, as Mary Magdalen met you in the garden on the morning of your resurrection, so may we meet you today and every day: Speak to us as you spoke to her; reveal yourself as the living Lord; renew our hope and kindle our joy; and send us to share the good news with others.

*Frank Colquhoun**

vi Dying you destroyed our death,
rising you restored our life.
Lord Jesus, come in glory. *ICEL*

187 Thanksgiving

Thanks be to you, O Christ, because you have broken for us the bonds of sin and brought us into fellowship with the Father.
Thanks be to you, O Christ, because you have triumphed over death, and opened to us the gates of eternal life.
Thanks be to you, O Christ, because where two or three are gathered together in your name, you are there among them.

Thanks be to you, O Christ, because you are alive for ever to intercede for us.
For these and all other benefits of your mighty resurrection, thanks be to you, O Christ.

*New Every Morning**

188 Christ's presence

We give you thanks, heavenly Father, for you have delivered us from the power of darkness, and brought us into the kingdom of your Son; grant that, as by his death he has recalled us to life, so by his continual presence in us he may raise us to eternal joy; through the same Christ our Lord.

Mozarabic Sacramentary

189 The Christian Passover

Almighty Father, who has made your Son to be our passover sacrifice that we may be freed from sin by his death and united with him by his resurrection; give us grace so to purge ourselves of the old yeast of evil and wickedness, that we may serve you in sincerity and truth; through Jesus Christ our Lord.

190 Those in need

Lord Christ, shine upon all who are in the darkness of suffering or grief; that in your light they may receive hope and courage, and in your presence may find their rest and peace; for your love's sake.

Alan Warren

191 At the end of Easter Day

O Lord, who by triumphing over the power of darkness prepared our place in the New Jerusalem; grant us, who have this day given thanks for your resurrection, to praise you in that city of which you are the light; where with the Father and the Holy Spirit you live and reign, now and for ever.

*William Bright**

(See also 35 and 36)

EASTER 1

192 Faith and doubt

Christ our Saviour, Son of the Father, crucified and alive for ever; grant to us the faith which doubts not your word, trusts where it cannot see, and rests in your love and mercy, now and for ever.

193 The last beatitude

O risen Christ, who said, 'Blessed are those who have not seen, and yet have believed'; grant that we, and all those who trust you without seeing you, may know and feel our fellowship with you, now and in the perfect vision of your glory, for you are alive and reign, our Lord and God, for ever.

194 Leaders

God, almighty Father, King of kings and Lord of all our rulers; grant that the hearts and minds of all who go out before us, the statesmen, the judges, the men of learning, and the men of wealth, may be so filled with the love of your laws, and of that which is righteous and life-giving, that they may serve as wholesome salt to the earth, and be worthy stewards of your good and perfect gifts; through Jesus Christ our Lord.

EASTER 2

195 Emmaeus

Make our hearts to burn within us, O Christ, as we walk with you in the way and listen to your words; that we may go in the strength of your presence and your truth all our journey through, and at its end behold you, in the glory of the eternal Trinity, God for ever and ever. *E. Milner-White**

196 Journeys

Ever loving Father, preserve us in our going out and our coming in, open our eyes to see you in the stranger we meet by the way, and on our last journey let us come safely into your eternal presence; through the love of Jesus Christ our Saviour. *F. Heald*

197 The Good Shepherd

Lord Jesus Christ, Good Shepherd who gave your life for the sheep; gather into your fold those who have wandered away, feed those who are hungry, give rest in green pastures to those who are weary of life, bind up the wounds of those who are injured, and strengthen those who are weak; guide us all in right pathways for your name's sake.

EASTER 3

198 The Easter message

God, through the mighty resurrection of your Son Jesus Christ you have liberated us from the power of darkness and brought us into the kingdom of your love; grant that as he was raised from the dead by the glory of the Father, so we may walk in newness of life, and look for those things which are in heaven, where with you, Father, and the Holy Spirit, he is alive and reigns for ever and ever.

Gelasian Sacramentary

199 Intercession

O God, creator and preserver of all mankind, bless the people of all nations: reconcile those who are divided, relieve the hungry and the oppressed, bring joy to the sorrowing, and peace and hope to all; through our Lord and Saviour Jesus Christ.

Revised Services of the Church of Ireland

200 The dead

Lord God, creator of all men, you have made us creatures of this earth, but have also promised us a share in eternal life. May all who have died share this eternal life with your saints in heaven, where there is neither sorrow nor pain, but life everlasting. We ask this through Christ our Lord.

A Christian's Prayer Book

EASTER 4

201 The Way, the Truth, and the Life

Lord Jesus Christ, the Way, the Truth, and the Life; let us not stray from you, the Way, nor distrust you, the Truth, nor rest in any other but you, the Life; teach us by your Holy Spirit what to believe, what to do, and in what to take our rest; we ask it for your name's sake. *Erasmus*

202 The Church

Lord God, heavenly Father, grant to your Church today the faith of her apostles, the hope of her martyrs, and the love of her Lord, even Jesus Christ, in whose name we pray. *Christopher Idle*

203 Co-operation

O God, you make men to be of one mind in an house and have called us into the fellowship of your dear Son; draw into closer unity the peoples of all races in this and every land, that, in fellowship with you, they may understand and help one another, and that, serving you, they may find their perfect freedom; through the same your Son Jesus Christ our Lord. *Joost de Blank*

EASTER 5

204 Inward peace

Lord Jesus Christ, you have promised that in you we may have peace, and have encouraged us by your victory over the world; give us ears to hear, and faith to receive, your word; that, in all the confusions and tensions of this present life, with mind serene and purpose stedfast, we may continue to abide in you, who died and rose again, and are alive for ever. *F. B. Macnutt**

205 The dead

Almighty God, the God of the spirits of all; multiply, we pray, to those who rest in Jesus the many blessings of your love; that the good work which you have begun in them may be perfected for the day of Jesus Christ: and, in your mercy, grant that we, who now serve you here on earth, may at the last, together with them, be found worthy to share the inheritance of the saints in light; for the sake of your Son, Jesus Christ our Saviour. *1928 Prayer Book**

206 After prayer

Grant, Lord, that we may live in your fear, die in your favour, rest in your peace, rise in your power and reign in your glory; for your own beloved Son's sake, Jesus Christ our Lord. *William Laud**

ROGATION DAYS

207 A collect

Loving Father, you promise to supply all our needs out of your abundant store; prosper the labours of those who enable us to enjoy the resources of nature, whether by farming, fishing, or industrial work, that we may render thanks and praise to you; through Jesus Christ our Lord.

Collects with the New Lectionary

208 Stewardship

Give, Lord, to all who till the ground wisdom to understand your laws, and to co-operate with your wise ordering of the world; and grant that the plentiful fruits of the earth may not be hoarded by the selfish nor squandered by the foolish, but that the needs of all men shall be supplied according to the new order of your kingdom; through Christ our Lord. *The Kingdom, the Power, and the Glory**

209 Disaster

God of goodness and love, in whom we can trust in every hour of need; have mercy on all who are faced with fear and distress (through earthquake, tempest, pestilence, flood. . .). We ask that help may be given to them speedily, and that this emergency may be turned into an opportunity to strengthen the bonds of love and service which bind men and nations together; through Jesus Christ our Lord.

Christian Aid

210 A blessing

May God the Father of our Lord Jesus Christ, who is the source of all goodness and growth, pour his blessing upon all things created, and upon us his children that we may use them to his glory and the welfare of all peoples; and the blessing. . .

Sarum Missal

ASCENSION DAY

211 Thanksgiving

Blessed are you, Lord God almighty, the Ancient of Days, for you have set your Son Jesus Christ our Lord upon the glorious throne of your kingdom, exalted far above all peoples, all places, all times, eternally; that he who has worn our nature and carried our humanity into the innermost sanctuary, should pour gifts from heaven upon his brothers, and be both our righteous judge and most merciful intercessor; to whom with you, Father, and you, Holy Spirit, one God, be given all might, majesty, power and praise, now and for ever.

*After the Third Collect**

212 The divine purpose

Almighty God, who, after your Son had ascended on high, sent forth your Spirit in the Church to draw all peoples to yourself; bring your promise to fulfilment, and, at the appointed time, gather together in one all things in heaven and on earth, into Christ who is head over all things in the Church, his body.

213 Christian unity

Father, we pray for your Church throughout the world, that it may share to the full in the work of your Son, revealing you to men and reconciling men to you and to one another; that Christians may learn to love one another and their neighbours, as you have loved us; that your Church may more and more reflect the unity which is your will and your gift; we pray through Jesus Christ our Lord.

Prayer from the Chapel of Unity, Coventry Cathedral

214 Freedom

Grant, O God, that, laying aside the sins which hinder the coming of your kingdom, the nations of the world may be assured of the right which you have given them to live in freedom: freedom from want and fear, freedom of thought and speech, and freedom to worship you according to your will; through Jesus Christ our Lord. *F. B. Macnutt**

(See also 22, 37 and 38)

THE SUNDAY AFTER ASCENSION DAY

215 The Renewal of the Church

God our Shepherd, give the Church a new vision and a new charity, new wisdom and fresh understanding, the revival of her brightness and the renewal of her unity; that the eternal message of your Son, undefiled by the traditions of men, may be hailed as the good news of the new age; through him who makes all things new, Jesus Christ our Lord. *Percy Dearmer**

216 The ordained ministry

Lord our God, you have chosen ministers to serve you in your Church, and have given them a perfect example in the person of your Son; pour your blessing on your servants, that by word and deed they may proclaim your saving love, and so enable all your people to grow up into Christ, who is our Lord and Head for ever and ever. *ACCM**

217 Dedication

Almighty God, in whom we live and move and have our being, you have made us for yourself, so that our hearts are restless until they rest in you; grant us purity of heart and strength of purpose, that no selfish passion may hinder us from knowing your will, no weakness from doing it; but that in your light we may see light clearly, and in your service find our perfect freedom; through Jesus Christ our Lord. *Saint Augustine*

PENTECOST

218 Thanksgiving

To you, O Christ, King exalted, we offer our sincere and heartfelt praise, for you have sent down and shed abroad your Holy Spirit to restore and renew the spirit of men, to be the first dedication of your Catholic Church on earth, and the first proclamation of the gospel to all nations, the bond of unity, and giver of light and life; to him, with the Father and you, one blessed Trinity, be given all might, majesty, power and praise, now and for ever.

*After the Third Collect**

219 The Holy Spirit

God, who in generous mercy sent upon your disciples the Holy Spirit in the burning fire of your love; grant that your people may be fervent in the fellowship of faith; so that, always abiding in you, they may be found stedfast in faith and active in service; through Jesus Christ our Lord. *Gelasian Sacramentary*

220 The Holy Spirit

Holy Spirit of God, who came upon our Lord Christ at the river Jordan, and upon the disciples at the feast of Pentecost; in your mercy give light to our minds and purity to our hearts; for the sake of Jesus Christ our Lord. *From Saint Nerses of Clajes*

221 Mission

O God, you have made of one blood all nations of men to dwell on the face of the earth, and sent your Son Jesus Christ to preach the good news of peace to those who are far away, and to those who are near at hand; grant that all the peoples of the world may feel after you and find you; and hasten the fulfilment of your promise to pour out your Spirit on all mankind; through Jesus Christ our Lord.

*G. E. L. Cotton**

222 Those in need

O God, your eye is over all the children of men, and you have called them into a kingdom not of this world; send your Holy Spirit into the dark places of life; May he still the noise of our strife and the turmoil of the peoples; may he give faith to the doubting, hope to the fearful, strength to the weak, confidence to the sick, and light to the mourners; through Jesus Christ our Lord. *James Martineau**

(See also 17, 39 and 40)

TRINITY SUNDAY

223 The Vision of God

Lord God almighty, you have given us the vision of your holiness, and thereby of our own unworthiness to be your witnesses; touch, we pray, our lips with your cleansing fire; that so cleansed and hallowed, we may go out into the world with the authority of your commission; for Jesus Christ's sake. *Daily Prayer**

224 The Queen and Government

Lord, the God of righteousness and truth, grant to our Queen and her government, to members of

Parliament and all in positions of responsibility, the guidance of your Spirit. May they never lead the nation wrongly through love of power, desire to please, or unworthy ideals, but always love righteousness and truth; so may your kingdom come and your name be hallowed; through Jesus Christ our Lord. *Book of Prayers for Students**

225 Praise

To God the Father who first loved us, and made us accepted in the beloved Son; to God the Son, who loved us and washed us from our sins in his own Blood; to God the Holy Spirit, who sheds abroad the love of God in our hearts; to the one true God be all love and all glory for time and for eternity.

Thomas Ken

PENTECOST 2

226 Before prayer

Eternal Light, illuminate us; eternal Power, strengthen us; eternal Wisdom, instruct us; eternal Mercy, have pity on us; and grant us with all our hearts and minds to seek your face, and to love your name; through Jesus Christ our Lord.

*William Bright**

227 Christian Unity

O God, whose will it is that all your children should be one in Christ; we pray for the unity of your Church. Pardon all our pride and our lack of faith, of understanding and of charity, which are the causes of our divisions. Deliver us from narrow-mindedness, from our bitterness, from our prejudices. Save us from considering as normal that which is a scandal to the world and an offence to your love. Teach us to recognise the gifts of grace among all those who call upon you and confess the faith of Jesus Christ our Lord.

Liturgy of the French Reformed Church

(See also 21)

228 Rulers and Statesmen

O God, by whose power alone men are enabled to live together as brothers; look upon the broken body of humanity, and grant that wherever men meet in council for the ordering of the world, your Holy Spirit may bring them into unity and lead them in the way of peace; through Jesus Christ our Lord. *New Every Morning**

PENTECOST 3

229 The Church's witness

Lord, make us more effective witnesses for the gospel and deepen our understanding of the faith; that our convictions may be so strong that we shall want to share them, and so lucid that we shall know how to communicate them; for the honour of our Lord Jesus Christ. *After Mervyn Stockwood*

230 Doubt

Most merciful God, we pray for those who doubt your love; for those who find it difficult to believe or to pray; for those who have lost a faith they once possessed. May the Holy Spirit enlighten their minds and lead them into all truth; through Jesus Christ our Lord. *Frank Colquhoun*

231 Death

Grant to us, O God, to trust you not for ourselves alone, but for those also whom we love and who are

hidden from us by the shadow of death; that, as we believe your power to have raised our Lord Jesus Christ from the dead, so we may trust your love to give eternal life to all who believe in him; through Jesus Christ our Lord.
(See also 26)

PENTECOST 4

232 Knowledge
Eternal God, the light of the minds that know you, the joy of the hearts that love you, and the strength of the wills that serve you; grant us so to know you that we may truly love you, and so to love you that we may fully serve you, whom to serve is perfect freedom, in Jesus Christ our Lord.
After Saint Augustine

233 Creation
We thank you, Lord of all creation, for the wonder of the world in which we live, for the earth and all that springs from it, and for the mystery of life and growth. We pray that our gratitude may be shown by our care to conserve the powers of the soil, by our readiness to learn from scientific research, and by our concern for a fair distribution of the earth's resources. We ask these things in the name of Christ our Lord.
Basil Naylor

234 The ordained ministry
Remember, Lord, the ministers of your Church for their work in word and sacrament, and in the proclamation of your glorious gospel. Endow them with wisdom for their high task, with learning for the publishing of your truth, with zeal and devotion to your glory and the salvation of all men, with

humble self-surrender lest they themselves be rejected; and grant that both by their lives and their work they may advance your kingdom; for the honour of your Son our Saviour Jesus Christ.

From the Liturgy of Saint James

PENTECOST 5

235 The Bible

O Lord, you have given us your word for a light to shine upon our path; grant us so to meditate on that word, and to follow its teaching, that we may find in it the light that shines more and more until the perfect day; through Jesus Christ our Lord.

Saint Jerome

236 The Church

O God, we pray for your Church which is set today amid the perplexities of a changing order and is face to face with a new task. Grant that, loyal to apostolic faith and order, it may interpret the gospel in terms relevant to the age, and as the fulfilment of the highest hopes and the deepest needs of every nation; so that all men may worship Christ as their Lord and Saviour, who is alive and reigns with you and the Holy Spirit, one God, now and for ever.

237 The Theatre

O God, the King of glory, who in the making of man bestowed on him the gift of tears and the sense of joy, and implanted in his nature the need for recreation of mind and body; give to those who minister to that need, through drama and music, in the calling of the theatrical profession, a high ideal, a pure intention and a due sense of responsibility. And both to them, and to those who accept their ministry, give the skill so to use it that it may be for the enrichment of human character, and for your greater glory; through Jesus Christ our Lord.

*Actors' Church Union**

PENTECOST 6

238 Spiritual sight

Almighty Father, whose blessed Son restored sight to the blind man who asked for mercy; clear away the blindness of our hearts, inform our minds with your truth, and lead us in the way of your Son to live to the praise of your glory; through Jesus Christ our Lord.

239 Charity

Lord Christ, Son of the living God, who at the last judgement will acknowledge all deeds of mercy as done to you; grant, in this world of sin and pain and want, that we may never pass by the poor and helpless whose cry is your own; for the honour of your holy name. *Daily Prayer*

240 Foreign Policy

God and Father of all, you have taught us to care for one another and to live in peace; grant that our policies towards other nations may be dictated not by self-interest but by concern for the common good, and that we may seek to further the cause of justice and freedom in the world; through Jesus Christ our Lord. *James M. Todd*

PENTECOST 7

241 Industrial peace and goodwill

Let us pray that all men may learn to seek first the Kingdom of God and his righteousness, caring for

justice more than for gain, and for fellowship more than for domination.
Let us pray that all have the courage and the energy to think for themselves strongly and clearly, and to seek for the truth and follow it whatever the cost.
Let us pray for deliverance from prejudice and for a desire to appreciate what is just and true in the opinions of those who differ from us.
Let us pray that all may have the faith to believe that whatever is right is always possible, and that what is according to the mind of Christ is upheld by the limitless resources of omnipotence.
Let us pray that in ourselves and in others suspicion may give place to trust, and bitterness to goodwill; and that we all become trustworthy, whether we work with hand or brain.
Let us pray that God will grant peace in our time, and give us abundantly of his Holy Spirit, whose fruits are love and joy and peace. *William Temple*

PENTECOST 8

242 Listening to the Spirit

All-powerful God, whose Spirit came upon us in signs of wind and fire; help us to throw off what hampers our service, and to stand and listen to the voice of the wind, so that we may be caught in its onward rush; through him who died and rose again that the Spirit might dwell in us.

After William Temple

243 The Gifts of the Spirit

God our Father, you send your gifts freely upon your children. Preserve us from envy and jealousy; teach us to rejoice in what others have and we have not, to delight in what they achieve and we cannot accomplish, to be glad in what they enjoy and we do not experience; fill us daily more completely with love; through Jesus Christ our Saviour.

William Knight

244 Prosperity

O God, who in your love has bestowed on us gifts such as our fathers never knew or dreamed of; in your mercy grant that we may be not so occupied with material things that we forget the things which are spiritual; lest, having gained the whole world, we lose our own soul; for your mercy's sake.

*Daily Prayer**

PENTECOST 9

245 The Christian War

God our Father, we are so weak and disinclined to undertake any good and daring work for you. We pray you to give us strength to fight the spiritual war bravely; support us against our negligence and cowardice, and preserve us from the treachery of our own faithlessness; for the sake of Jesus Christ our Lord. *After Saint Augustine*

246 The Kingdom of Christ

O God, by your Son Jesus Christ you have set on earth a kingdom of holiness to measure its strength against all others; make faith to prevail over fear, and righteousness over force, and truth over the lie, and love and concord over all things; through Jesus Christ our Lord. *War Prayers 1940**

247 Persecution

O God, Father of all mercies, give to all Christian people courage to confess your name. In your mercy strengthen those who are being persecuted for their witness to your gospel, so that, as they stand fast for your holy word, they may be sustained by it; through Jesus Christ our Lord.

After Prayers of 1585

PENTECOST 10

248 The Washing of Feet

Jesus, Lord and Master, who served your disciples in washing their feet; serve us often, serve us daily, in washing our motives, our ambitions, our actions; that we may share with you in your mission to the world and serve others gladly for your sake; to whom be glory for ever. *After Michael Ramsey*

249 The spirit of service

O God, our heavenly Father, whose Son our Lord Jesus Christ took the form of a servant and became the Man for others; give to us the same spirit of service and help us to follow in his steps, that with love and humility we may give ourselves to those who need our help; for the glory of your name.

Frank Colquhoun

250 Caring professions

Lord, Son of Man, you have taught us that in serving others we are serving you; we pray for all who serve in agencies of care and relief; encourage them in times of disappointment, frustration and weariness, so that by their work mankind may be renewed in your image.

PENTECOST 11

251 The service of God

Blessing and honour, and thanksgiving and praise,

more than we can utter, more than we can conceive, be yours, holy and glorious Trinity, Father, Son and Holy Spirit, by all angels, all men, all creatures, for ever and ever. *Lancelot Andrewes**

252 The service of man

Give to your Church, O God, the grace to follow in the steps of Jesus, who came among us as one who serves. May it be ready in all the world to spend and be spent in the service of the poor and hungry, the sick and the ignorant. May it work with strength and suffer with courage for the liberation of the oppressed and the restoration to all men of the dignity and freedom of those created in your image. Grant this, our Father, for the sake of the same Jesus Christ our Lord. *John Kingsnorth*

253 Music

Eternal Lord God, source of all beauty and harmony, we praise you for the gift of music: for the inspiration given to those who compose it, for the skill and devotion of those who perform it, for the faculties and powers which enable us to enjoy it; and we pray that, as by the gift our lives are enriched and renewed, so we may glorify you in a fuller dedication of ourselves, giving thanks always for all things in the name of our Lord Jesus Christ.

Frank Colquhoun

PENTECOST 12

254 The witness of the Church

Eternal God and Father, give to us and to all your people grace and courage to proclaim your mighty work in Christ, in the crib and on the cross and in the world today. May we work together for the coming of the kingdom in our own time, ever looking in joyful hope for its consummation at the end of the age; through Jesus Christ our Lord.

John Kingsnorth

255 All nations

God and Father of mankind, who in your love made all the nations of the world to be one family; help those of different races to love and understand one another better. Take away hatred, jealousy and prejudice, so that all may work together for the coming of your kingdom of righteousness and peace; through Jesus Christ our Lord.

After Evelyn Underhill

256 Selection and training for ministry

God our Father, by the power of your Spirit you call and equip your people for the work of ministry in the Body of your Son; guide those who have the responsibility of discerning where you would have each of us serve you; and bless the work of those who, through their teaching and example, prepare men and women for ministry, that the Church may be strengthened and your kingdom enlarged. We ask this in the name of Jesus Christ our Lord.

PENTECOST 13

257 Persecution

Lord God, the refuge and strength of your people in every hour of need; sustain all who suffer for their allegiance to the faith of Christ. Give them courage and patience to endure to the end; that by their example and witness they may win others to the service of him who suffered for all mankind, our Saviour Jesus Christ.

Contemporary Parish Prayers adapted from Worship Now

258 At peace with all men

God the Father of our Lord Jesus Christ, the Prince of peace; grant us meekness and patience, that, preserved from the spirit of revenge, we may show to those who wrong us generosity and love; through Jesus Christ our Lord.

259 Hospitals

O God, the Father of mankind, to whom alone is known the mystery of suffering; hear our prayers on behalf of those in hospital who are bearing the burden of sickness or pain, or have to undergo an operation. In their weakness and anxiety draw near to them with your comfort and strength, and give them the assurance that, sharing their suffering, you will also share with them your peace, in Jesus Christ our Lord. *Prayers for use in Hospitals**

PENTECOST 14

260 Family Life

Father of all, accept our thanks for the joys of family life. Help us to live so that we may strengthen and enrich the life of the family. Help us to build with you the kind of family which welcomes the stranger, the lonely and the needy. Teach us through this small family to love the family of all mankind and to realise our part in it. In the name of Christ we ask this. *Brother John Charles, SSF*

261 Broken homes

Father in heaven, pattern of all parenthood and lover of children, we pray for homes and families across the world (*or* in this community). Sustain and comfort them in need and sorrow. In times of bitterness, tension and division, draw near to heal.

May parents and children together be learners in the school of Christ, daily increasing in mutual respect and understanding, in tolerance and patience, and in all-prevailing love; through Jesus Christ our Lord. *Timothy Dudley-Smith*

262 Marriage Guidance Counsellors

O God, our Father, whose Son our Lord blessed the marriage at Cana in Galilee by his presence and the first of his miracles; hear our prayer for all who seek to counsel those whose marriages are at risk. Give them sympathy, understanding, and insight into the needs of others; and so use them in this service that, by your grace, hurts may be healed, faults forgiven, and misunderstandings removed. We ask this prayer in the name of Jesus Christ our Saviour.

Llewellyn Cumings

PENTECOST 15

263 Government

Sovereign Lord of men and nations, we pray for rulers and statesmen who are called to leadership among their fellow countrymen; give them vision to see far into the issues of their time, courage to uphold what they believe to be right, and integrity in their words and motives; and may their service to their people promote the welfare and peace of mankind; through Jesus Christ our Lord.

Basil Naylor

264 Justice

God, mighty and merciful, the judge of all men; grant to those who minister justice the spirit of wisdom and discernment; and, that they may be strong and patient, upright and compassionate, fill them, we pray, with the spirit of your holy fear; through Jesus Christ our Lord. *J. Armitage Robinson**

265 The nation

Grant, O God, your protection; and in your protection, strength; and in strength, understanding; and in understanding, knowledge; and in knowledge, the knowledge of justice; and in the knowledge of justice, the love of it; and in that love, the love of existence; and in the love of all existence, the love of God, God and all goodness. *Ancient Welsh Prayer*

PENTECOST 16

266 Responsibility for mission

O Lord, you have warned us that you will require much of those to whom much is given; may we, who enjoy so rich an inheritance of faith, work together the more fruitfully, by our prayers, our labours and our gifts, to share with those who do not know you what we so plentifully enjoy; and, as we have entered into the labours of others, so to work that others may enter into ours, to the fulfilment of your will and the salvation of all mankind; through Jesus Christ our Lord. *Fifth century Prayer*

267 Social Services

Heavenly Father, whose Son visited mankind in all its suffering and need, and went about doing good; inspire with your love and compassion those engaged in social work in this town (*or* district). Encourage them when the tasks seem overwhelming. Give them wisdom when situations seem insoluble. Challenge them when they are tempted to pass by on the other side. And help them to show their love for you by their love for their neighbour; through Jesus Christ our Lord. *Michael Botting*

268 Prisoners

We pray, our Father, for those whose freedom has been taken from them: for all who suffer imprisonment, whether for crime or for conscience' sake; for all whose vision of your world is seen through bars, and in whose heart the lamp of hope burns low. God of mercy, give them help, according to their need, and hear our prayer for Jesus Christ's sake.

Timothy Dudley-Smith

PENTECOST 17

269 The changelessness of God

Father of all light, with whom there is no variation, no shadow caused by change; give us grace to rest upon your eternal changelessness, and in your faithfulness to find peace; through Jesus Christ, who is the same today as he was yesterday, and as he will be for ever. *Daily Prayer**

270 Words and actions

Make us careful, O Lord our God, to consider our actions before we do them, and our words before we speak them, whether they be good or bad, kindly or cruel, honest or deceitful, generous or mean; that there be none that you will not approve, and we shall repent: for Jesus Christ's sake.

271 Economic justice

Heavenly Father, may your Holy Spirit lead the rich nations to support the poor, and the strong nations to protect the weak; so that every nation may develop in its own way, and work together with other nations in true partnership for the promotion of peace and the good of all mankind; through Jesus Christ our Lord. *Diocese of Melanesia*

PENTECOST 18

272 The tongue

Set a guard, Lord, upon our tongues, that we may never speak the cruel word which is not true; or being true, is not the whole truth; or being wholly true, is merciless; for the love of Jesus Christ our Lord. *Daily Prayer**

273 Sharing

Make us ever eager, O Lord, to share the good things that you give us. Grant us such a measure of your Spirit that we may find more joy in giving than in getting. Make us ready to give cheerfully without grudging, secretly without praise, and in sincerity without looking for gratitude. For Jesus Christ's sake. *John Hunter**

274 Work

O God, the creator of all things, you have made man in your own image, so that he must ever seek his joy in creative work; have mercy, we pray, on all who are unemployed, or whose work is dull; and help us so to order our common life that every man may have work to do and find joy in doing it, to the good of this nation and the glory of your name; through Jesus Christ our Lord. *New Every Morning*

PENTECOST 19

275 Faith, hope and love

Lord God, perfect in us what is lacking in your gifts; of faith to increase it, of hope to establish it, of love to kindle it; and make us to fear but one thing only, the fearing of anything more than you, our Father, our Saviour, our Lord, for ever and ever.

After Lancelot Andrewes

276 Conflict

O God, you have bound us together in a common life. Help us, in the midst of our struggles for justice and truth, to confront one another without hatred or bitterness, and to work together with mutual forbearance and respect, through Jesus Christ our Lord. *ECUSA Book of Common Prayer*

277 The Civil Service

We pray, O God, for those who hold office in the life of this country (*or* place), and for all who in various ways serve the community; that fulfilling their duties with singleness of purpose, they may wisely and faithfully exercise the authority committed to them and promote the common good; through Jesus Christ our Lord. *Frank Colquhoun*

PENTECOST 20

278 Perseverance

Teach us, good Lord, to serve you as you deserve; to give and not to count the cost; to fight and not to heed the wounds; to toil and not to seek for rest; to labour and not to ask for any reward, save that of knowing that we do your will; through Jesus Christ our Lord. *Saint Ignatius Loyola*

279 Christian Unity

Lord, pour upon us the fullness of your mercy, and by the power of your Spirit remove divisions among Christians. Let your Church become a sign for all the nations, that the world may be filled with the light and joy of your Spirit, and believe in Jesus Christ whom you have sent, who is alive and reigns with you and the Holy Spirit, one God, now and for ever.

280 The Armed Forces

O God our Father, we pray for all who serve in the Forces. May they meet danger with courage, and all occasions with discipline and loyalty. Save them from the spirit of cruelty and revenge, that they may truly serve the cause of justice and peace; for the honour of your name.

PENTECOST 21

281 The Kingdom of Christ

Father of light and God of all truth, purge the world of all errors, abuses, corruptions and sins. Let humility triumph over pride, charity over hatred, meekness over passion, generosity over greed, and let the Gospel of Christ in faith and practice liberate the world; for he is now alive and reigns with you and the Holy Spirit, God for ever and ever.

*Percy Dearmer**

282 Christian Unity

Lord Jesus Christ, who prayed for your disciples that they might be one, even as you are one with the Father; draw us to yourself, that in common love and obedience to you we may be united to one another, in the fellowship of the one Spirit, that the world may believe that you are Lord, to the glory of God the Father. *William Temple*

283 The Bereaved

O God, the Lord of life, the conqueror of death, our help in every time of trouble, you do not willingly grieve or afflict your children; strengthen those who mourn, and give us grace, in the presence of death, to worship you, that we may have sure hope of eternal life, and put our whole trust in your goodness and mercy; through Jesus Christ our Lord.

PENTECOST 22

284 Decision

O Lord the only wise, the God and Father of all, you have shown to man light and darkness, right and wrong, that he may choose freely between them; grant us both generosity and courage to choose the good and to refuse the evil, that we may be numbered among your sons in whom you are well pleased, and who dwell in your presence; through Jesus Christ our Lord.

285 Students

Grant, Lord, to all students, to love that which is worth loving, to know that which is worth knowing, to praise that which pleases you most, to esteem that which is most precious to you, and to dislike that which is evil in your eyes. Grant that with true judgement they may distinguish between things that differ, and, above all, may search out and do what is well-pleasing to you; through Jesus Christ our Lord. *Thomas à Kempis*

286 Commerce

God, our heavenly Father, guide with your Holy Spirit those who direct the commercial life of the nation(s). Grant them to look on their life's work as an opportunity of service rather than of gain; fill them with jealous care of their employees; and so bless them that we may all benefit from their labours; for the sake of Jesus Christ our Lord.

Peter Green

PENTECOST 23

287 Knowledge

Good Jesus, you have deigned to refresh our souls with the sweet streams of knowledge; grant that one day we may come to you, its source and spring.

Alcuin

288 Citizens of heaven

Eternal God, our heavenly Father, you have given to your servants an abiding citizenship in heaven, and, in the days of our pilgrimage, a citizenship also upon earth; help us, as we journey to that heavenly city, so faithfully to discharge the duties which fall upon us on our way, that we may be found ready for the full vision of your glory; through Jesus Christ our Lord.

*Daily Prayer**

289 Social Justice

Almighty God, you have entrusted this earth to the children of men, and through your Son Jesus Christ have called us to a heavenly citizenship; grant us such shame and repentance for the disorder, injustice and cruelty which are among us, that, fleeing to you for pardon and grace, we may henceforth set ourselves to establish that city which has justice for its foundation and love for its law, of which you are the architect and builder; through the same Jesus Christ, your Son, our Saviour.

William Temple

THE DEDICATION FESTIVAL

290 The Parish Church

God our heavenly Father, make the door of our parish Church wide enough to receive all who need human love and fellowship and a Father's care, and narrow enough to shut out all envy, pride, and lack of love; here may the tempted find help, the sorrowing receive comfort, the careless be awakened to repentance, and the penitent be assured of your mercy; and here may all your children renew their strength and go on their way in hope and joy; through Jesus Christ our Lord.

291 The Parish Church

God our Father, we thank you for this house of prayer in which you bless your family on its pilgrimage. So quicken our consciences by your holiness, nourish our minds by your truth, purify our imaginations by your beauty, and open our hearts to your love, that, in the surrender of our wills to your purpose, the world may be renewed in Christ Jesus our Lord. *After William Temple*

292 Dedication

Go with us, Lord, as we enter your holy house; and go with us as we return to take up the common duties of life. In worship and in work alike may we know your presence near us, till work itself be worship, and our every thought be to your praise; through Jesus Christ our Lord. *Daily Prayer**

293 Our parish

God bless this church and parish, and prosper all our attempts to be faithful and to draw others to you, for Jesus Christ's sake. *Old Scottish Prayer*

REMEMBRANCE SUNDAY

294 Act of Remembrance

Let us remember before God, and commend to his sure keeping:

those who have died for their country in war;
those whom we knew, and whose memory we treasure;
those who have lived and died in the service of mankind.

Those to be remembered may be named.

They shall not grow old as we that are left grow old:
age shall not weary them, nor the years condemn.
At the going down of the sun and in the morning
we will remember them.
We will remember them.

The Silence is observed. Then may be sounded the Last Post and Reveille.

Almighty and eternal God, from whose love in Christ we cannot be parted, either by death or life: hear our prayers and thanksgivings for all whom we remember this day: fulfil in them the purpose of your love; and bring us all, with them, to your eternal joy; through Jesus Christ our Lord.

A Service for Remembrance Sunday 1968

295 Intercession

i Let us pray for the peace of the world:
for statesmen and rulers that they may have wisdom to know and courage to do what is right. . .
for all who work to improve international relationships that they may find the true way to reconcile people of different race, colour, and creed. . .
for men and women the world over that they may have justice and freedom, and live in security and peace. . .

Silence may be kept.

Lord, in your mercy,
Hear our prayer.

Most gracious God and Father, in whose will is our peace; turn our hearts and the hearts of all men to yourself, that by the power of your Spirit the peace which is founded on righteousness may be established throughout the world; through Jesus Christ our Lord.

ii Let us pray for all who suffer as a result of war:
for the injured and the disabled,
for the mentally distressed,
and for those whose faith in God and in man has been weakened or destroyed. . .
for the homeless and refugees,
for those who are hungry,
and for all who have lost their livelihood and security. . .
for those who mourn their dead,
for those who have lost husband or wife, children or parents, and especially for those who have no hope in Christ to sustain them in their grief. . .

Silence may be kept.

Lord, in your mercy,
Hear our prayer.

Almighty God, our heavenly Father, infinite in wisdom, love and power; have compassion on those for whom we pray; and help us to use all suffering in the cause of your kingdom; through him who gave himself for us on the cross, Jesus Christ your Son, our Lord. *A Service for Remembrance Sunday 1968*

Saints' Days

296 King Charles the Martyr (January 30)
Heavenly Father, your faithful servant Charles prayed for those who executed him; by his example teach us to love and bless our enemies through the power of the Holy Spirit and the intercession of our Lord and Saviour Jesus Christ.

297 The Presentation of Christ in the Temple
(February 2)

The Blessing of Candles and the Procession

The congregation gather with unlighted candles. A hymn may be sung, and the candles are lit. After a brief word of introduction the candles are blessed:

God our Father, whose Son was revealed to Simeon as the light of the nations, and the glory of Israel; let these candles + be to us a sign of his light and presence, that, guided by your Holy Spirit, we may live by the light of faith until we come to the light of glory; through Christ our Lord. *Amen.* *David Silk*

During the procession Nunc Dimittis, or a suitable hymn, is sung. When this ceremony precedes the Eucharist, it is appropriate to begin with the Gloria in excelsis. The candles may be taken home after the service, and lit as a sign of welcome to Christ.

298 Polycarp of Smyrna (February 23)
Almighty God, you gave to your servant Polycarp boldness to confess the Name of our Saviour Jesus Christ before the rulers of this world, and courage to die for this faith; grant that we may always be ready to give a reason for the hope that is in us, and to suffer gladly for the sake of our Lord Jesus Christ.

ECUSA, The Book of Common Prayer

(This prayer is suitable for other saints, and in times of persecution.)

299 **David, Patron Saint of Wales** (March 1)
God our Father, you gave the bishop David to the Welsh Church to uphold the faith and to be an example of Christian perfection. In this changing world may his example help us to hold fast to the values which bring eternal life; through Jesus Christ our Lord. *Roman Missal**

300 **Patrick, Patron Saint of Ireland.** (March 17)
Almighty God, in your providence you chose your servant Patrick to be the apostle of the Irish people, and to bring those who were wandering in darkness and error to the true light and knowledge of your word; keep us in that light, and bring us to everlasting life; through Jesus Christ our Lord.
Revised Services of the Church of Ireland

301 **George, Patron Saint of England** (April 23)
Lord, hear the prayers of those who praise your mighty power. As Saint George followed Christ in suffering and death, so may he help us in our weakness; through Jesus Christ our Lord, who is alive and reigns with you and the Holy Spirit, one God, now and for ever. *Roman Missal*

302 **Alban, first martyr of Britain** (June 22)
Father, by your grace Saint Alban gave himself up for his friend, and was the first in this land to shed his blood for Christ. May we, after his example, endure all suffering for the love of you, and seek you with all our hearts, for you alone are the source of life; through Jesus Christ our Lord. *Roman Missal*

303 **Thomas More** (July 6)
Lord, strengthen us by the example of your martyr Thomas, so that we may always follow conscience,

and be the king's good servant, but God's first; through Jesus Christ our Lord.
(This prayer may be adapted for a variety of occasions)

304 The Beheading of Saint John the Baptist (August 29)
Almighty God, who called your servant John the Baptist to be the forerunner of your Son in birth and death; strengthen us by your grace, that, as he suffered for the truth, so we may boldly resist corruption and vice and receive with him the unfading crown of glory; through Jesus Christ our Lord.
Collects, Alternative Services, Series Three

305 Francis of Assisi (October 4)
God our Father, by your gift Saint Francis followed Christ in poverty and humility; may we, after his example, serve you without faltering, and come with joy to the riches of eternal life; through Jesus Christ our Lord. *David Silk*
(This prayer is suitable for other religious)

306 The Conception of the Blessed Virgin Mary (December 8)
Merciful God, hear the prayers of your people who commemorate the Conception of the Mother of the Lord; and grant that, as with her we look for his first coming as our Saviour, so we may be ready to greet him when he comes again as our Judge; for he is now alive and reigns with you and the Holy Spirit, one God, now and for ever. *David Silk*

307 Blessings
God grant to the living, grace; to the departed, rest; to the Church, the Queen, the commonwealth, and all mankind, peace and concord; and to us and all his servants, life everlasting; and the blessing. . .
Based on a sixteenth century prayer

308 May the Lord of his great mercy bless you, and give you understanding of his wisdom and grace;
May he nourish you with the riches of the Catholic Faith, and make you persevere in all good works;
May he keep your steps from wandering, and direct you into the paths of love and peace;
And may the blessing. . . *Southwark Diocese**

309 Go in peace: may the love of the Father enfold you, the wisdom of the Son enlighten you, and the fire of the Spirit kindle you: and may the blessing of the Lord God come down upon you, and remain with you always.

Private Devotion

These prayers are traditionally used in the first person singular, but may easily be adapted to the plural, or in other ways, for general use.

310 Anima Christi

Soul of Christ, sanctify me,
Body of Christ, save me,
Blood of Christ, refresh me,
Water from the side of Christ, wash me,
Passion of Christ, strengthen me,
O good Jesus, hear me,
Within your wounds hide me.
Let me never be separated from you,
From the powers of darkness defend me,
In the hour of my death call me,
And bid me come to you,
That with your saints I may praise you
For ever and ever. Amen.

311 Act of self-oblation

Lord Jesus Christ,
take all my freedom,
my memory, my understanding, and my will.
All that I have and cherish,
you have given me.
I surrender it all to be guided by your will.
Your grace and your love are wealth enough for me.
Give me these, Lord Jesus,
and I ask for nothing more. *Saint Ignatius Loyola*

312 Act of devotion

My God, I am not my own but yours.
Take me for your own,
and help me in all things to do your holy will.

My God, I give myself to you,
in joy and in sorrow,
in sickness and in health,
in success and in failure,
in life and in death,
in time and for eternity.
Make me and keep me your own;
through Jesus Christ our Lord.

313 God be in my head

God be in my head,
and in my understanding;
God be in my eyes,
and in my looking;
God be in my mouth,
and in my speaking;
God be in my heart,
and in my thinking;
God be at my end,
and at my departing.

Sarum Primer

314 The 'Jesus Prayer'

Lord Jesus Christ, Son of God,
have mercy on me, a sinner.

THE EUCHARIST

THE EUCHARIST

There is provision in the Alternative Service Book for the minister to use 'appropriate' or 'suitable' words other than those provided.

THE GREETINGS

315 The grace of our Lord Jesus Christ and the love of God and the fellowship of the Holy Spirit be with you all;
and also with you.

316 The grace and peace of God our Father and the Lord Jesus Christ be with you;
and also with you.

THE INVITATION TO CONFESSION

317 Seeing we have a great high priest who has passed into the heavens, Jesus the Son of God, let us draw near with a true heart, in full assurance of faith, and make our confession to our heavenly Father.
Holy Communion, Alternative Services, Series Two
The introduction to the Confession at Morning and Evening Prayer is also suitable.

THE INTERCESSION

i In the form provided in the service itself, specific needs may be included, either by inserting subjects between the paragraphs, in which case they should take the form of address to God, or by prefatory biddings, in which case they should take the form of address to the congregation.

The response may be used before or after the insertions.

It is essential to the broad sweep of the prayer that insertions or biddings should be brief, or they will tend to duplicate the prayer itself. On a typical occasion the intentions of the congregation might be expressed as follows:

(a) We pray for *(N)* and for all those to be ordained with him next Sunday; and for the work of the Church in . . .

We offer our concern for the government and people of . . .; and for the staff and students of . . . University.

We give you thanks for our families, and for all on whom we depend for the necessities of life; we remember especially those who will take exams this week.

Hear our prayers for . . . and all who are sick; be with their families, and guide their doctors.

We remember . . . and all who have died recently, and . . ., whose anniversaries fall today; and we ask you to sustain those who mourn them.

Each petition is followed by a short period of reflection, and the response, or the response is said after the set text.

(b) Let us pray for *(N)* and for all those to be ordained with him next Sunday; and for the work of the Church in . . .

For the government and people of . . .; and for the staff and students of . . . University.

Let us remember our families and those on

whom we depend for the necessities of life, and pray especially for those who will sit exams this week.

Our prayers are also asked for . . . and all who are sick; we remember, too, their families and those who tend them.

Of your Christian love pray for . . . and for all who have died in faith.

Let us pray for the Church and for the world . . .

Each bidding is said slowly and thoughtfully, with time for reflection, and then the prayer is said as a continuous whole, or interspersed with the responses.

ii **The General Intercession** (in the appendix) may be used in the same way as the form in the service.

iii **The Litany** (in the appendix) may be used with biddings only; but these may precede the prayer, or be inserted before each of the three sections.

iv The provision for other suitable forms of prayer makes possible the use of many of the prayers in the earlier part of this book, introduced by biddings; or litanies (such as that provided for the Easter Vigil); or biddings followed by the response; or a period of free prayer in which anyone present may participate; or silence.

Other forms of Intercession

318 Almighty God, who has taught us to make prayers and intercessions for all men:
We pray for the clergy, and for all who guide the thoughts of the people; for artists, authors, musicians, and journalists; that our common life may be crowned with truth and beauty;

For all who heal the body, guard the health of the nation, and tend the sick; that they may follow the footsteps of Christ, the great physician;
For all on whose labour we depend for the necessities of life; for all who carry on the commerce of the world, that they may seek no private gain which would hinder the good of all;
For parents and children; that purity, love, and honour may dwell in our homes, and duty and affection may be the bond of our family life;
For all who draw near to death, that they may know your presence with them through the valley of the shadow and may wake to the vision of your glory; through Jesus Christ our Lord.

*John Hunter**

319 Almighty and everliving God, hear the prayers which we offer in faith;
For peace and for the salvation of all men,
Lord, in your mercy,
Hear our prayer.
For the one holy catholic and apostolic Church, and for the unity of all Christian people,
Lord, in your mercy,
Hear our prayer.
For bishops, priests and deacons, and especially for *N* our bishop,
Lord, in your mercy,
Hear our prayer.
For those who learn and those who teach the Christian faith,
Lord, in your mercy,
Hear our prayer.
For all who live and work in this parish,
Lord, in your mercy,
Hear our prayer.

For families and for those who live alone,
Lord, in your mercy,
Hear our prayer.
For the sick and afflicted,
Lord, in your mercy,
Hear our prayer.
For all in authority, and especially for Elizabeth our Queen,
Lord, in your mercy,
Hear our prayer.
For those who work for peace, justice and righteousness throughout the world,
Lord, in your mercy,
Hear our prayer.
For . . .
Lord, in your mercy,
Hear our prayer.
Mindful of the holy apostles and martyrs, and of all your servants departed this life in your faith and fear, we commend ourselves, and one another, and our whole life to you, Lord God, through Jesus Christ our Saviour.

Revised Services of the Church of Ireland

320 The leader makes the following biddings, and in the course of the pause which follows the people may mention subjects for prayer.

I ask your prayers for God's family throughout the world, for all who bear responsibility among his people, for all ministers of the word and sacraments, and for all who gather in his name here in . . .

Silence

I ask your prayers for the peace of the world, for the rulers of all the nations, for government in accordance with God's holy will, and for a just and proper use of the natural resources of the world.

Silence

I ask your prayers for the concerns and activities of this congregation and of this neighbourhood, for ourselves, our families, friends and neighbours.

Silence

I ask your prayers for all in sorrow, need, anxiety or sickness, for the neglected, the persecuted and the lonely, and for those in need or trouble.

Silence

Let us praise God for those in every generation in whom Christ has been honoured, and pray that we also, inspired by their example, may have grace to glorify Christ.

Silence

Almighty God, to whom our needs are known before we ask, help us to ask only what accords with your will; and those good things which we dare not or in our blindness cannot ask, grant us for the sake of your Son, Jesus Christ our Lord.

ECUSA, Book of Common Prayer

(See also number 184)

THE PREPARATION OF THE GIFTS

At the preparation of the gifts the president is allowed freedom to praise God in his own words, the people responding:

Blessed be God for ever.

321 The Bread

Blessed are you, Lord, God of all creation.
Through your goodness we have this bread to offer,
which earth has given and human hands have made.
It will become for us the bread of life.
Blessed be God for ever. *ICEL*

322 The Wine

Blessed are you, Lord, God of all creation.
Through your goodness we have this wine to offer,
fruit of the vine and work of human hands.

It will become our spiritual drink.
Blessed be God for ever. *ICEL*

AFTER COMMUNION

323 Before Advent

Almighty God, by your gift the tree of life was set at the heart of the earthly paradise, and the Bread of Life was set at the heart of your Church; let this divine nourishment bring us, not to judgement, but to life eternal; through Christ our Lord.

324 Advent

God our Father, whose Son was born into the world to free us from sin and death, and to bring us to everlasting life; purify us by this his perfect sacrifice, that, when he comes in power and glory, we may greet him without shame or fear; through the same Christ our Lord. *David Silk*

325 Christmas

Almighty God, you have shed upon us the new light of your incarnate Word; Let that light, rekindled by this eucharist, shine forth in our lives; through Jesus Christ our Lord. *David Silk*

326 Lent

Lord, God of our fathers, you feed your children with the true manna, the living Bread from heaven; let this holy food support us through our earthly pilgrimage until we come to the place where there is neither hunger nor thirst; through Christ our Lord.

327 Passiontide

Lord, we have celebrated the memorial of your Son's eternal sacrifice; by his passion guard and defend us; by his wounds heal us; by his blood wash us from sin; by his death bring us to everlasting glory; for in him is the end of our aspirations and desires, now and for ever.

328 Easter

Father, your risen Son was recognised by his disciples in the breaking of bread; through the power of this same blessed sacrament of his presence, may we abide with him, and he with us; for he is alive and reigns for ever. *David Silk*

329 Ascension

God our Father, as by your grace you have raised us up in union with Christ Jesus and given us a place with him in heaven, so help us to devote ourselves to the good deeds for which you have designed us; through Christ our Lord. *David Silk*

330 Pentecost

O God, in this eucharist you have united us in the bond of peace; deepen our communion one with another in Christ, and grant that, through the work of your Spirit within us, we may daily increase in the knowledge of your love, and learn to love our brethren with the love you have shown in Jesus Christ our Lord. *Adapted from Response*

331 The Saints

O God, in this eucharist you have brought us near to an innumerable company of angels, and to the spirits of just men made perfect; as in this food of our earthly pilgrimage we have shared their fellowship, so may we come to share their joy in heaven; through Christ our Lord.

332 We thank you, Lord, that you have fed us in this sacrament, united us with Christ, and given us a foretaste of the heavenly banquet prepared for all mankind. *The Methodist Service Book*

333 We thank you, holy Father, for your holy name, which you have made to dwell in our hearts, and for the knowledge, faith and immortality which you have made known to us through your servant Jesus: to you be glory for ever. *Didache*

334 We give you thanks, Father, for this holy meal in which Christ is received, the memory of his passion is renewed, our lives are filled with grace, and a pledge of future glory is given us. To him with you and the Holy Spirit be glory for ever. *Roman Breviary*

335 Strengthen for service, Lord, the hands that have taken holy things; may the ears which have heard your word be deaf to clamour and dispute; may the tongues which have sung your praise be free from deceit; may the eyes which have seen the tokens of your love shine with the light of hope; and may the bodies which have been fed with your body be refreshed with the fulness of your life; glory to you for ever. *Liturgy of Malabar*

336 God our Father, whose Son, the light unfailing, has come from heaven to deliver the world from the darkness of ignorance; let these holy mysteries open the eyes of our understanding that we may know the way of life, and walk in it without stumbling; through the same Christ our Lord.

337 Lord God, whose Son is the true vine and the source of life, ever giving himself that the world might live; may we so receive within ourselves the power of his immortal sacrifice, that, in this cup of his life, we may share his glory and be made perfect in his love, for he is alive and reigns with you and the Holy Spirit, God, now and for ever.

THANKSGIVINGS

At a service without Communion the minister should say the service as far as the Absolution, and then add the Lord's Prayer, the General Thanksgiving, and other prayers at his discretion. Alternative seasonal thanksgivings are to be found earlier in this book. General Thanksgivings follow here.

338 Let us give thanks to the Lord:
For his mercy and love are everlasting.

Father, through Jesus Christ and in the power of your Holy Spirit, receive our thanksgiving:
For the creation of the universe through your Word,
For making man in your image and likeness,
For the revelation of your purposes through the law and the prophets,
We give you thanks and praise.

For the gift of your Son, Jesus Christ our Lord,
For his lowly birth of Mary and for his baptism in the Jordan,
For his ministry of preaching, teaching and healing,
We give you thanks and praise.

For his steadfast love in going to Jerusalem,
For his agony in the garden of Gethsemane,
For his suffering and death on the cross,
We give you thanks and praise.

For his resurrection from the dead and his ascension to your right hand in glory,
For his eternal intercession for us,
For his promise of his coming again to be our judge,
We give you thanks and praise.

For the outpouring of your Spirit on the Church,
For the commissioning of your Church to make disciples,
For the spreading of your kingdom throughout the world,
We give you thanks and praise.

Here special thanksgivings may be offered.

We give you thanks and praise.

So, Father, we give you grateful thanks for all your blessings, and
We offer you our souls and bodies
To be a living sacrifice.
Send us out in the power of your Spirit
To live and work to your praise and glory.
Amen. *The Methodist Service Book**

339 We thank you, heavenly Father, for all your goodness to us and to all men.
For the world in which you have placed us, with its wonder and beauty. For life and health, for food and clothing, for kind friends and happy homes. For those who love us, and for all who have shown in their lives a good example. Most of all, for Jesus Christ, your only Son our Saviour, who came into the world and died for us on the cross, and rose again from the dead, and is now our Friend in heaven.
With him, and in him, and through him, by the power of the Holy Spirit, with all who stand before you in earth and heaven, we worship you, Father, in songs of everlasting praise:
Blessing and honour and glory and power be yours for ever and ever. Amen.

*Church of Scotland Book of Common Order**

OCCASIONAL OFFICES

OCCASIONAL OFFICES

BAPTISM AND CONFIRMATION

There is no rubrical permission for other prayers at these services. It is permitted to omit the Prayers of Penitence and the Intercession, although intercessions may be introduced by appropriate biddings before the prayers. Alternatively it is possible either to use the Litany at the entrance procession or the procession to the Font. The absence of intercession is probably most evident when Baptism is administered at the Parish Eucharist and the congregation needs to retain its continuing intercessory life despite the demand for brevity and the dramatic connection between the act of Baptism and the Peace. A simple expedient is for the parish priest to address the congregation immediately after the opening greeting. Such a brief bidding, which includes the minimum of parochial and other needs, is then summed up in the Kyrie Eleison and the collect. Alternatively, a bidding might be said before or after the sermon.

MARRIAGE

There is provision in the Marriage Service for other prayers.

340 O gracious and merciful Father, by whose appointment marriage has been given to the human race, and by whose blessing it is strengthened and sustained; we pray for N and N, now joined as husband and wife. Keep them loyal and steadfast to each other. May their love know no doubt or change, but may shared tasks, trials, and joys bind them ever more closely in heart; through Jesus Christ our Lord. *Worship Now*

341 O God, whose Son, Jesus Christ, shared at Nazareth the life of an earthly home, we pray that he may be acknowledged as head of the household of these your children. And, as he found his authority in serving, so may they learn to serve one another in love. We remember, too, the homes from which they have come, and pray that you will bless those who have given them to each other; through Jesus Christ our Lord. *Worship Now*

342 O God, by whom, in the Gospel, we are all invited to the marriage supper of your Son, so incline the hearts of these your servants that they may give obedience to your call. Bring them, at the end of their days, to your banqueting house, and may your banner over them be always love; through Jesus Christ our Lord. *Worship Now*

343 Most holy and merciful God, by whom the solitary are set in families, we pray that your blessing may remain with N and N, now joined in your name. May their marriage be for them a source of great and lasting good. Spare them long to each other, and keep them faithful, tender and true, so that they may live together in peace and holiness. In prosperity may they be grateful to you, the giver of all good; in trouble may they find that you are their refuge and their strength. So lead them through this life, we pray, that when they have fully served you in their generation, they may be received into the presence of your glory; through Jesus Christ our Lord. *Worship Now*

FUNERALS

344 Thanksgiving for the departed
Almighty and merciful Father, we give you thanks for the life of your child N; and we pray that, preserving the good of his example among us, you will guard your truth from generation to generation; through Jesus Christ our Lord.
*Funeral Service, Alternative Services, Series Two**

345 The Contakion

Give rest, O Christ, to your servant with your saints: where sorrow and pain are no more; neither sighing, but life everlasting.
You alone are immortal, the creator and maker of man; and we are mortal, formed from the earth, and to the earth we shall return; for you so ordained when you created us, saying, Dust you are, and to dust you shall return; we shall all go down to the dust; and, weeping over the grave, we sing alleluia, alleluia, alleluia.
Give rest, O Christ, to your servant with your saints: where sorrow and pain are no more; neither sighing, but life everlasting. *Russian Liturgy*

346 A holy death

Grant, O God, that in our sorrow for the departure from this world of your son/daughter N, we may always remember that we are most certainly to follow him/her. Give us grace to prepare for that last hour by a good life, that we may not be surprised by a sudden and unprepared death, but be ever vigilant, so that, when you call us, we may be ready to enter into eternal glory; through Christ our Lord.

347 The Bereaved

O Lord Jesus Christ, God of all consolation, whose heart was moved to tears at the grave of Lazarus; look with compassion on your children in their loss. Strengthen in them the gift of faith, and give to their troubled hearts, and to the hearts of all men, the light of hope, that they may live as one day to be united again, where tears shall be wiped away, in the kingdom of your love; for you died and were raised to life with the Father and the Holy Spirit, God, now and for ever.

PASTORAL OFFICES AND PRAYERS

PASTORAL OFFICES AND PRAYERS

A LITANY FOR THE QUEEN AND COMMONWEALTH

348 Let us pray.
Heavenly Father, we give you thanks for the wonder of creation, for the gifts of human life and for the blessing of human fellowship;
for Christ, your living Word;
through whom we are taught the perfect way of life and the royalty of service, and for your Spirit, who offers his gifts to us for the common good.
We thank you, Lord.

For the blessing of community in our Nation and Commonwealth, and for those who have used your gifts to strengthen and enrich its life;
We thank you, Lord.

We give you thanks for our Sovereign Lady, Queen Elizabeth, and for her family;
for her long and tireless service to our world-wide family of nations;
for her profession of faith in you by word and deed;
for her example and unselfish devotion and duty;
for her care for her people, and her concern for them at all times and in all places;
We thank you, Lord.

Continue in her and her family, we pray, your royal gifts of service;
the vision of your will for her people;
wisdom to fulfil her vocation of leadership in a Commonwealth of many races;
strength and courage to carry out the duties of her calling;

and grant her always the assurance of your presence, your power, and your love.
Lord, in your mercy
Hear our prayer.

We pray for the people of the Commonwealth and their governments;
for those called to lead them through the crises of our times, through racial and social tensions.
Lord, in your mercy
Hear our prayer.

In the Church's ministry of the Gospel, for a clear message of your love and power,
Lord, in your mercy
Hear our prayer.

In national and local government, for insight, integrity and courage,
Lord, in your mercy
Hear our prayer.

In the administration of law and in the defence of our people, for justice and humility, fairness and compassion,
Lord, in your mercy,
Hear our prayer.

In industry and commerce, in trade and business, for mutual care and co-operation and a concern for all men's good,
Lord, in your mercy,
Hear our prayer.

In art and music, theatre and entertainment, sport and leisure, for recognition that all gifts come from you to give to one another,
Lord, in your mercy,
Hear our prayer.

In every mode of communication, in literature and press, radio and television,
for a vision of social good and for service to the truth,
Lord, in your mercy,
Hear our prayer.

In education, in family and school, in college and training schemes, for a concern not only with information but also with maturity and fulfilment of life,
Lord, in your mercy,
Hear our prayer.

In the service of those in need and sickness, anxiety and suffering, for a community that cares,
Lord, in your mercy,
Hear our prayer. *Service for the Silver Jubilee*

A LITANY FOR THE PARISH

349 Help us with your grace, good Lord, to live as true followers of your Son Jesus Christ:
Grant this, O Lord.

That in all things we may hold to your will and purpose:
Grant this, O Lord.

That our hearts and minds may be open to your holiness and truth:
Grant this, O Lord.

That we may rightly value the whole of your creation:
Grant this, O Lord.

That we may seek your righteousness in all our dealings with one another:
Grant this, O Lord.

That we may bear each other's burdens, and so obey your law:
Grant this, O Lord.

That we may maintain and set forward love and peace among all men:
Grant this, O Lord.

That we may bring comfort to the lonely, strength to the fearful, wisdom to the ignorant, and a living hope to those who walk in darkness:
Grant this, O Lord.

That in all our time on earth we may work and live as citizens of your heavenly kingdom:
Grant this, O Lord.

Lord, in your mercy hear and receive these our prayers, which we offer in the name of your blessed Son, Jesus Christ our Lord.
Amen. *Daily Prayers, General Synod*

RENEWAL OF MARRIAGE VOWS

This material can be used during the Eucharist, or provided with a ministry of the word, and prayers.

(Dear friends in Christ), God is the loving Father of the world of nature and of the new creation of grace. In marriage he brings together the two orders of creation and re-creation, just as, day by day, the bread and wine we offer become the Body and Blood of his Son. Today we gather to give thanks for the enrichment of our lives through marriage, and to pray for a renewal by the Holy Spirit of the grace of Christian marriage.

350 Collect

Father, you have made the bond of marriage a holy mystery, a sign of Christ's love for his Church. With faith in you and each other, we pledge again our love, and pray that our lives may ever bear witness to your divine love in the world; through Jesus Christ our Lord, who is alive and reigns with you and the Holy Spirit, one God, now and for ever.

David Silk

351 The Vows

God has consecrated us in Baptism, and has strengthened us by marriage. We now renew our vows, and pray the Lord to deepen our love and increase our faith. Will you join your right hands, and say after me:

I renew my vow to you
to have and to hold
for better for worse
for richer for poorer
in sickness and in health
to love and to cherish
till death us do part.

Rings may be blessed:

In your name, Lord, we dedicate these rings; and we pray that these your children may keep true faith one with another, and remain in unbroken love to their lives' end.

The rings are exchanged.

I give you this ring
in token of my constant faith
and abiding love
in Christ Jesus our Lord.
Amen.

Prayers from the Marriage Service may be used.

SERVICE AFTER A CIVIL MARRIAGE

If it is inappropriate to use the Marriage Service, the following may be used:

Penitence

In the name of the Father, and of the Son, and of the Holy Spirit.
Amen.

The Lord be with you;
and also with you.

We have come together in the presence of God our Father to share the joy of N and N in their marriage, to thank him for his goodness, to confess our sins, and to pray that their union may be a sign of his love in the world. Let us therefore confess our sins to him.

352 **i** *Most merciful God, we have sinned in thought, and word, and deed:*
we are truly sorry and we ask you to forgive.
Help us by your Spirit to live the new life in Christ,
loving you with all heart, and our neighbour as ourselves;
for Jesus Christ's sake. Amen.

Cyril Taylor and David Silk

ii Almighty God forgive us our sins, and keep us in life eternal. *Amen.*

The Word of God

353 Almighty God, Lord of all life and giver of all joy, Grant that N and N in simple trust, may commit themselves to your keeping and, by your grace, may live together in mutual love and faithfulness; through Jesus Christ our Lord, who is alive and reigns with you and the Holy Spirit, one God, now and for ever.

1. Corinthians 13.
Psalm 37. 3–7.
John 2. 1–11.
An address may be given.

The Prayers

354 Let us pray with confidence to God our Father, the author and giver of all good things.
Grant that N and N may be loyal and faithful to each other, supporting each other throughout their life, may they bear each other's burdens and share each other's joys.
Lord, in your mercy
Hear our prayer.

May they be honest and patient with each other, recognising and acknowledging their faults, and seeking each other's forgiveness and yours:
Lord, in your mercy
Hear our prayer.

(Give them wisdom and understanding in the care of children, that their home may be an image of your kingdom:
Lord, in your mercy
Hear our prayer.)

Give them such fulfilment of their mutual affection that they may reach out in love and concern for others:
Lord, in your mercy
Hear our prayer.

Keep them faithful to you, and at the end of this life on earth, receive them and us into your eternal kingdom;
We make these prayers through Jesus Christ our Lord, who taught us to say:
Our Father . . .

Blessing

The Lord bless you and protect you;
The Lord smile on you and show you his favour;
The Lord befriend you and give you his peace.

THE DEDICATION OF GIFTS

When memorial gifts are to be dedicated, they are first offered in a thanksgiving prayer and then dedicated:

355 i Blessed are you, Lord, God of all creation; through your goodness we have this/these gift(s) to offer, the fruit of the skills you have given us. Accept it/them, and us, to further your purpose in the world.
Blessed be God for ever.

ii In the Faith of Christ, and for the benefit of his holy Church, we dedicate this. . . to the glory of God (and in memory of his son/daughter N); in the name of the Father, and of the Son, and of the Holy Spirit.
Amen. *After the Third Collect**

(Other prayers may follow for the donor and for the purpose of the gift(s).)

THE BLESSING OF A HOUSE

ON ENTERING THE HOUSE:

Peace be to this house;
And to all who dwell in it.

356 Visit this house, O Lord, and drive from it all that is evil. Defend from harm all who pass through this door, and bless them in their going out and coming in; through Jesus Christ our Lord.
Amen.

IN A BEDROOM:

In peace I will lie down and sleep;
For you alone, Lord, make me dwell in safety.

357 O Lord God, our heavenly Father, you neither slumber nor sleep: Guard with your unfailing watchfulness all who take their rest here, that, refreshed by the gift of sleep, they may serve you joyfully day by day; through Jesus Christ our Lord.

IN A CHILD'S ROOM:

Jesus said: Let the children come to me, do not hinder them;
For to such belongs the kingdom of God.

358 Almighty God, our heavenly Father, whose blessed Son shared at Nazareth the life of an earthly home; make your love known to the children who shall live here, and give wisdom and understanding to those who have the care of them, that they may grow into the pattern of your Son Jesus Christ.

IN THE KITCHEN:

Jesus said: Which is the greater, one who sits at table, or one who serves?
But I am among you as one who serves.

359 Lord, grant to all who shall work in this room that, in serving others, they may serve you, and share in your perfect service, and that, in the noise and clutter of the kitchen, they may possess you in peace; through Jesus Christ our Lord.

AT THE DINING TABLE:

360 God, you give good things liberally and grudge not: may all who shall eat and drink together at this table be joined in true friendship and praise you with thankful hearts; through Jesus Christ our Lord.

IN THE LIVING ROOM:

Jesus entered a certain village;
And a woman named Martha received him into her house.

361 O God, whose blessed Son has said: I have called you friends: Unite in true fellowship and love all who shall use this room; through Jesus Christ our Lord.

Then is celebrated the Eucharist, beginning at the Peace. If this is not appropriate, the Lord's Prayer is said.

The Blessing:

362 Lord, Bless +, Hallow +, and Sanctify + this house, that in it there may be charity, peace, humility, kindness, gentleness, health, obedience and thanksgiving to the Father, Son, and Holy Spirit; and let your blessing come down on those who dwell in it, now and for ever.

THE BLESSING OF WATER

363 God our Father, your gift of water brings life and freshness to the earth; it washes away our sins and brings eternal life. Bless and hallow + this water, renew the living spring of your life within us, and protect us in spirit and body, that we may be free from sin and serve you in purity of heart; through Christ our Lord.

EPILOGUE

EPILOGUE

364 Union with God

O God, of your goodness, give us yourself, for only in you do we have all. *Julian of Norwich*

365 Stability

God almighty, Father of our Lord Jesus Christ, by the gift of your Spirit establish and ground us in your truth. Reveal to us what we do not know; perfect in us what is lacking; strengthen in us what we know; and keep us in your service without fault; through the same Jesus Christ our Lord.

Saint Clement of Rome

366 Intercession

God the Father, and the eternal High Priest Jesus Christ, build us up in faith and love, and grant us part among the saints with all those who believe in our Lord Jesus Christ. We pray for all Christian people, for rulers and leaders, for the enemies of the cross of Christ; and for ourselves we pray that our fruit may be abundant, and that we may be made perfect in Christ our Lord. *Saint Polycarp of Smyrna*

367 Blessing

May the infinite and glorious Trinity, the Father, the Son, and the Holy Spirit, direct our life in good works, and after our journey through this world, grant us eternal rest with the saints.

Mozarabic Sacramentary

ACKNOWLEDGEMENTS

The Editor wishes to express his thanks to the following for permission to reproduce or adapt material of which they are the authors, publishers, or copyright holders.

BBC Publications for four (adapted) prayers from *New Every Morning*.

The Church of Scotland for one prayer (adapted) from the *Book of Common Order* (1940).

The Saint Andrew Press for five prayers from *Worship Now*, compiled by D. Cairns, I. Pitt-Watson, J. A. Whyte, T. B. Honeyman.

Eight prayers (adapted) from *Daily Prayer*, edited by Eric Milner-White and G. W. Briggs (1941); one prayer (adapted) from *The Kingdom, The Power and the Glory* (4th ed. 1934); and one prayer from *The Book of Common Prayer set forth by authority for use in the Church of the Province of South Africa* (1954) reprinted by permission of Oxford University Press.

The Church Missionary Society for one prayer (adapted) from *With All our Strength*.

The Student Christian Movement Press for one prayer from *A Book of Prayers for Students* (4th ed. 1923), p. 153; and for one prayer from *Student Prayer* (1950), p. 157.

The Actors' Church Union for one prayer.

The Bishop of Norwich for one prayer.

One prayer (adapted) from *Response* published by Forward Movement Publications, Cincinnati, Ohio, USA.

Two prayers from *Collects with the New Lectionary* by P. R. Akehurst and A. J. Bishop, reprinted by permission of Grove Books, Bramcote, Nottingham.

Three prayers from Christian Aid's *Caring for God's World* (1971) compiled by Geoffrey Hyder and Tony Hodgson.

The Dean of King's College, Cambridge, for the *Christmas Bidding Prayer* (adapted).

The Bishop of Southwark for a prayer adapted from a diocesan letter; and for a blessing.

The Secretary-General of the General Synod of the Church of England for a litany from *Daily Prayers*.

Darton, Longman & Todd for a prayer from *A Catholic Prayer Book*.

Two prayers from *A Christian's Prayer Book*, edited by P. Coughlan, R. C. D. Jasper, and T. Rodrigues printed by permission of Geoffrey Chapman, a division of Cassell Ltd.

The Central Board of Finance of the Church of England for three prayers from ACCM prayer leaflets.

Text of six prayers from *The Book of Common Prayer* (Proposed), copyright 1977 reprinted by permission of Charles Mortimer Guilbert as Custodian of the Standard Book of Common Prayer. All rights reserved.

Extracts from the Silver Jubilee Service and the Royal Maundy Service, which are copyright, and extracts from *The Book of Common Prayer*, which is Crown Copyright, are included with permission.

The Methodist Publishing House for two prayers from the *Methodist Service Book*; and for one prayer (adapted) from the *Book of Offices*.

The Standing Committee of the General Synod of the Church of Ireland for four prayers from *Revised Services* (1973).

Excerpts from the English translation of *The Roman Missal* © 1973, International Committee on English in the Liturgy Inc. All rights reserved.

Hodder & Stoughton Ltd for twenty prayers from *Parish Prayers*; and thirty-four prayers from *Contemporary Parish Prayers*.

The Church Literature Association for *The Blessing of the Crib and Prayers at the Crib*.

The Joint Council of the Chapel of Unity, Coventry Cathedral, for *The Prayer of Christian Unity*.

The Moderator of the Church of South India for one prayer (adapted) from the *Book of Common Worship*.

The Prayers for St David and St George from the *Roman Missal* © 1974, The National Liturgical Commission of England and Wales.

The Publications Committee of the Episcopal Church in Scotland for a litany from the 1929 *Prayer Book of the Scottish Episcopal Church*.

The Society for Promoting Christian Knowledge for eleven prayers (adapted) from *A Procession of Passion Prayers* by Eric Milner-White; for two prayers from *A Service of Remembrance Sunday*; for a prayer by Miss A. Milne from *Ember Prayer*; and for the Order (adapted) for the *Blessing of a House*.

SPCK on behalf of the Joint Liturgical Group for prayers from the *Blessing and Procession of Palms* and the *Service of Light*.

Mowbray's Publishing Division for three prayers and a litany (adapted) from *The Priest's Book of Private Devotion*; two prayers by Brother John

Charles, SSF; three prayers (adapted) from *The Prayer Manual* compiled by F. B. MacNutt; and five prayers (adapted) from *After the Third Collect* edited by Eric Milner-White.

If the Editor has unwittingly transgressed any copyright, he makes sincere apologies and will acknowledge any such oversights in future editions.

INDEX OF SOURCES

(References are to prayer numbers)

INDEX OF SUBJECTS 1

(References are to prayer numbers)

INDEX OF SUBJECTS 2

(References are to prayer numbers)

This index, which is not exhaustive, may be useful for those compiling a group of prayers for a retreat, quiet day or conducted meditation.

INTERCESSION

NOTES

NOTES

NOTES